Hope: The Christian Response to Chicken Little

Hope: The Christian Response to Chicken Little

Robert E. Lauder

Fides/Claretian
Notre Dame, Indiana 46556

The quotations by Charles Peguy are from *God Speaks,* translated by Julian Green. Copyright 1943, 1954 by Pantheon Books. Reprinted by permission of Pantheon Books, a division of Random House, Inc.

Library of Congress Cataloging in Publication Data

Lauder, Robert E
   Hope, the Christian response to Chicken Little.

   1. Hope.   2. Lauder, Robert E.   I. Title.
BV4638.L37   248.4   80-10261
ISBN 0-8190-0636-X

To Diane and Jeanne with Hope and Love

Grateful acknowledgement is made to *The Long Island Catholic* for some material which appeared in its pages.

Contents

Introduction

This book is personal in a special sense. It is difficult for me to assess my faith or my love. But it is and has been clear to me for a long time that the virtue that must become more operative in me as I try to live the life of a Christian and especially as I try to live the life of a priestly minister is the virtue of hope. Seeing this need in my own life, I placed other projects into the background for a time and decided to focus my attention and reflections on the meaning of hope. This book is the result of those reflections. It has been written in the belief that what is deeply personal not only is not most private and individual but rather tends to be most universal and to have the most widespread application. My own struggles with hope, trust, and confidence I find mirrored in the lives of my friends and acquaintances. While the popular song "What the World Needs Now Is Love, Sweet Love" is true, the world could also use some hope. All of us could.

The virtues of faith, hope, and charity are operative and interactive in the life of a person who is open to God. In these reflections on hope I don't wish to so isolate the virtue of hope from personal Christian existence as to make hope abstract and lifeless like a branch fallen from a tree. Throughout these reflections the person who hopes is our main interest—the believing, loving person who, in spite of all sorts of evidence that seems to weigh against him is able to hope. Remarks about the meaning and mystery of person which may seem to be straying from the main topic of hope are really deeper probings into hope. To probe the mystery of person is to see the need for hope; to hope is to become a person.

This book might easily have been called *Hope: Personal Presence and Promise*. It wasn't, not because *Christian* replaces *personal* but because Christian in a special way incarnates and deepens the meaning of personal. The Christian is aware of special promises that enable him to hope. The Christian's hope is itself a kind of promise and a way of being present. That way of being present that we call hope, perhaps even more than love, sums up what it means to be a person and to be a Christian.

Person Explosion

There has been some kind of a "person-explosion." It's been going on for some time. On various levels of society, among people of enormously different backgrounds, there is an intense interest in the meaning, dignity, and importance of persons. A large portion of the human community has achieved a new sensitivity and appreciation of what it means to be a person. However, many cannot articulate that awareness nor communicate that appreciation. At times the awareness and appreciation seem to have come at too great a cost. To some people a whole world of traditions and values seems to be the price if the implications of the "person-explosion" are followed. I appreciate their fears. The tapestry of our lives seems to need reweaving. Somehow it's come undone. Something's been lost.

Much that once excited us now leaves us cold. Not only has much of the past become unglued but the present is increasingly confusing and the future less and less inviting. Is the hope of "putting it all together" a viable dream or a nightmare that will lead only to deeper frustration?

The problems that plague us are many, both in number and in type. Easy solutions are rightly suspect. What seems desperately needed is a direction, some basic truth or truths that will point us out of the woods toward a clearing. The various crises that threaten us, though they range from the threat of nuclear war to the breakdown of family life, are ultimately crises of meaning. Is there some radical meaning that can help us make more sense of the chaos that passes for contemporary living? I believe that the meaning that must be focused on if human living is going to be somehow hope-filled is the meaning of human person. It is precisely this meaning, this sense of self, that we seem to have lost. If the richness of the meaning of human person is going to be seen some understanding of hope must be grasped.

I am not suggesting that all problems will disappear or even be easily solved once a vision of person is clearly perceived; I am suggesting that inadequate or false views of person make solutions less likely if not impossible. I am also suggesting that within the meaning of person, if anywhere, are the seeds to solve each human problem. At the roots of our restlessness is a radical need for a personal vision of who we are, why we are, and where we are going. Essential to this personal vision is the virtue of hope. I believe that at this point in time such a vision is available, but it will be useless unless we make it our vision by grasping it as strongly as we can and understanding it as deeply as possible. It is no little thing to take the meaning of person seriously and to allow that meaning to transform all human relationships and indeed all human living.

Knowledge of Self

Exploring the meaning of person is a strange business. In trying to articulate what it means to be a person, we are involved in a search. It is the strangest search because we are looking for that which should be most evident and yet at the same time is most elusive. We are searching for our selves. Examining the meaning of person is a little frightening because to some extent our meaning is unknown to us. The examination is also exciting because it is an adventure into the most important area of reality: the self.

There is an obvious reason why we shouldn't expect the search to be difficult. If there is one reality which I know or at least ought to know, it is my self. I am present to my self in a way that I am not present to anything else. I have, so to speak, an inside view of a self. However, because the self is such a unique kind of reality, such a different type of being, because the way I am present to my self is so deeply mysterious, the search is far from easy. With the possible exception of the search for God, there is no search as demanding or as difficult as the search for the meaning of person. Grasping the meaning of my self is no easy task.

Besides being present to my self, I am absent from my self. Just the fact that I can write such a sentence suggests something of the strangeness of the search. I am present to my self because I am who I am. I know my self better than anyone else knows me, though occasionally my best friends surprise me and reveal to me a dimension of my self that was previously unknown by me. Though I know my self better than I know any other reality, though I am present to my inmost activities, to my daily routine, to my inmost thoughts and best kept secrets, I can't seem to penetrate to the core of my person. My self is not totally clear to me. I become aware that I am absent from my self through varied human experiences. I wonder why I perform certain actions. Even more disturbing to me is the fact that I have difficulty expressing my deepest thoughts and needs. I can't put myself into words. I find it very hard to tell people who I really am. I find it difficult to know who I am. There seems to be a layer of clouds that covers the core of my being, a mist that conceals me from myself or conceals myself from me.

Believing that we are being called to enter more deeply into the great mystery present within us, I choose to be hopeful concerning the future of persons. In trying to grow as a person I must hope. Though I strongly affirm that I am a person, I realize that personal reality is a very mysterious type of reality. All talk about personal existence will be speech grasping for a perfect expression, words straining to articulate what is beyond their capacity to express. Because a person is sacred, the search is important and even holy. Because a person is a mystery, the search will never end. That is, it will never end until hope is completely fulfilled.

1 Hope and the Presence of God

The Christian believer as he looks back on his life tends to see the hand of God providentially directing various happenings and events. Frequently he will be heard to say something like, "Ten years ago when that happened to me I thought nothing worse could have happened. But now as I think about it I see that it was a blessing in disguise. God was trying to teach me something." Of course the non-believer sees all such interpretations and "insights" as a brand of wishful thinking. Claiming that the believer by his interpretation of reality is predisposed to discover the activity of God everywhere, the nonbeliever settles for more immediate and obvious explanations and interpretations of events. Neither the believer nor the nonbeliever can prove his own position nor disprove the position of the other. Each gambles his life on his view of personal existence: the believer risks his life on the presence of God, the nonbeliever risks his life on the belief that the human is all that there is. Each makes a commitment based on his view of reality and tries to live by it. Very much related to the Christian's interpretation of reality, in fact at the heart of the Christian's interpretation of reality, is the virtue of hope. There is nothing like hope allowed in the nonbeliever's vision. The virtue of hope involves an Other, and by claiming that humanity is all that there is the nonbeliever has excluded the possibility of this Other.

An incident from my own life can serve as an example of how hope is central to the Christian's interpretation of reality and indeed how hope can color the believer's vision of what others might see as ordinary everyday human events. The example will serve to introduce us to the meaning of hope and the meanings hope can unveil. The incident goes back thirty years to when I was in eighth grade of grammar school. Though I had been accepted into a tuition-free high school, there was another high school, Xavier in Manhattan, that I wanted to attend even more than the tuition-free school. When I, with a couple of thousand other eighth grade students took the entrance test for Xavier I thought I had done quite well, perhaps even well enough to win a scholarship. However a few weeks after the exam I received notice that I had been accepted but no scholarship. This meant that I would attend the tuition-free school rather than Xavier. The matter seemed settled. But not for me. I kept praying that I would win a scholarship to Xavier, even though this seemed impossible since the notices had been sent out. I remember that my parents said to me that there was no point in hoping for a scholarship now. It was too late. I understood that but replied "God can do anything." I hoped, somehow, that God would work things out and I kept praying confidently. My hope must have been quite strong at that time. Well, God did work things out. Weeks later I received a letter from Xavier explaining that I had attained seventh highest grade in the entrance exam but because only six scholarships had been given out I was not originally a scholarship winner. Hence the earlier letter that informed me that I had been accepted. However one of the six scholarship students had decided to attend another high school and so I was awarded a scholarship.

God's Providence

What to make of the incident? For the nonbeliever the entire story can be explained simply. A bright eighth grade student won a scholarship and because of his beliefs tends to read the presence of God somehow operative in the whole process. The nonbeliever is partly correct: I do see the presence of God somehow operative in the whole process. I don't know whether I can be more precise than that. I am not claiming that God worked a miracle in the strict sense of the term—that he intervened and changed the grade on my exam. I know that all the evidence indicated that I had not won a scholarship, that I placed my trust completely in God and that after everyone else had given up hope I won. Putting that experience into the context of the four years I spent at Xavier High School I am convinced that God was directing my life. The influence of Xavier on me was enormous. To a large extent my high school years, for better or worse, made me who I am.

A few months ago I attended the twenty-fifth reunion of my high school graduation class. Every year the school in Manhattan has a Communion Supper to which all the alumni are invited. Each year the twenty-fifth and fiftieth anniversary classes are honored. For me the reunion was a marvelous mirror of life's mysteries. My experience of being a student at Xavier was filled with generous, dedicated teachers and priests. A few months ago as I joked and reminisced with former classmates, my high school experience seemed very near. Could twenty-five years have gone by so quickly? A lifetime, no matter how long, is very short. Being at the reunion I was reminded that my life has been blessed by the presence of some marvelous people.

Having returned to Xavier for the reunion I see the incident of the entrance exam in even broader perspective. Deciding to attend Xavier changed my whole life. The people I met, the teachers I had, the retreats I made, all these and other experiences have made me the person I am. If I hadn't gone to Xavier I would have a different life, be a vastly different person.

Let's focus in on my hope that I would win a scholarship and try to make some sense of it. After I took the exam, the fact is I came in seventh. Weeks later as I, ignorant of my score, hopefully prayed to God and placed my future in his hands the fact that I came in seventh had already occurred and was not changed by my prayers. However as I hopefully prayed I was in the dark, not knowing how God might work things out. This I think is the key: when we hope we are in the dark and we don't know how God will work things out but we hope and trust that he will. This is what is crucial about hope: we rely on God because we can't attain the goal by ourselves. What is important about the entrance exam incident is not that I received what I wanted or that I was able to go to the school I chose but that having done everything I could I placed myself in God's hands. In other words even if I hadn't won the scholarship, I hope I would continue to believe that God was operative in my life because he was and is. The advantage of my example is not the details but the truth underlying it: God never forgets, God never leaves, God never abandons us. Looking back on my high school experience I believe I can clearly see God's presence and his continued response to my hope. If my life had gone in a very different direction God would still be present. Maybe I would be able to discover his presence, maybe I wouldn't. The important truth is he would be present!

Job's Suffering and the Mystery of God

Instead of the encouraging example I have offered from my own life, let's look at a well-known example that at least on first appearance may not seem encouraging: the story of Job. Numerous hardships happen to Job. His friends presume that these hardships must be due to some sin that Job has committed. We often feel the same way in similar situations. "What did I do wrong that God allowed this to happen to me?" expresses a sentiment that we find too frequently among religious people. But Job is innocent, he hasn't committed any sin. Job's mistake is that he thinks his innocence should excuse him from all suffering. Job considers the human relationship with God in terms of justice: because Job has done God's will, God should do Job's will. But this is to misunderstand the relationship between God and his creatures. Near the end of the book God speaks to Job and indicates the correct relationship between creature and Creator. The sacred writer has God say

Who is this obscuring my designs
   with his empty-headed words?
Brace yourself like a fighter;
   now it is my turn to ask questions and yours to inform
     me.
Where were you when I laid the earth's foundations?
   Tell me, since you are so well informed!
Who decided the dimensions of it, do you know?
   Or who stretched the measuring line across it?
What supports its pillars at their bases?
   Who laid its cornerstone
when all the stars of the morning were singing with joy,
   and the Sons of God in chorus were chanting praise?

Who pent up the sea behind closed doors
    when it leaped tumultuous out of the womb,
when I wrapped it in a robe of mist
    and made black clouds its swaddling bands;
when I marked the bounds it was not to cross
    and made it fast with a bolted gate?
Come thus far, I said, and no further:
    here your proud waves shall break.

God goes on to point out the marvels of creation and to indicate how inferior man is to his creator. It is this God in whom we trust. Our hope must be in God's will for us not in our will for ourselves.

Two scenes from the New Testament come to mind that make the points similar to the message of the Book of Job. In trying to teach his apostles (Luke 17:7–10) about their relationship with God, Jesus told them:

    Which of you, with a servant plowing or minding sheep, would say to him when he returned from the fields, "Come and have your meal immediately?" Would he not be more likely to say, "Get my supper laid; make yourself tidy and wait on me while I eat and drink. You can eat and drink yourself afterward?" Must he be grateful to the servant for doing what he was told? So with you: when you have done all you have been told to do, say, "We are merely servants: we have done no more than our duty."

Jesus is trying to get the apostles to sense the awesomeness and greatness of his Father. An even more striking example of how our hope should be placed in our Father is provided in the story in John's gospel (9: 1–3) when Jesus' disciples ask him about the man born blind. "His disciples asked him 'Rabbi, who sinned, this man or his parents, for him to have been born blind?' 'Neither he nor his parents sinned', Jesus answered, 'he was born blind so that the works of God might be displayed in him'." The last phrase of Jesus "that the works of God might be displayed" pretty much sums up the focus our hope should have. Our Father loves us. At times we get clear indications, such as Jesus healing the blind man, but at other times our hope has to operate in a dark room. We hope that God is present with us but no immediate visible sign may be available. Ultimately the Christian has to rely on the sign of Jonah. Perhaps the most marvelous aspect of my entrance exam experience and my experience in high school is that they provide small signs that call my attention to the most important sign of God's love, the death and resurrection of Jesus. In this is our hope.

2 Hope: A Way of Being Present

The aspect of personhood that is especially helpful in shedding light on both the meaning of hope and the new meanings in our life that hope can help us unveil is the notion of personal presence. The mystery of personal presence is central to grasping the meaning of hope.

Presence and Personal Responsibility

A person is responsible for his presence. Where he spends his time opens up a whole set of worlds to him. How much of his time he spends in one area and the way he spends that time deeply affects the dimension of his worlds. Two simple examples may help. Let's imagine one person who spends most of his conscious hours in a library reading and doing research and another person who spends most of his day playing tennis. The first person may become a great scholar. He may become an extremely proficient reader and a person who is very much at home with books and ideas. In a way that is not true for most persons, he will be at home in the world of books. In a special way that world will be his turf, his home ground, a territory that is familiar to him. By putting his presence so intensely into the library world the person has access to meanings from books that the more casual reader or the less demanding student and researcher will not be able to grasp. However, that person places his presence so intensely into the library world that he pays for that presence in relation to other worlds. To a large extent the athletic world, the recreational world, and the social world will be closed to him. A similar analysis can be offered concerning the tennis player. He will excel in the athletic world of tennis, but he may be hopeless in the intellectual world. The next idea he has may be his first. He probably will be awkward and uncomfortable in the social world. A person is responsible for his presence.

Where, when, and *how* a person is present enormously influences the meaning of the world in which a person exists. The *how* of personal presence is especially important. It sheds the most light on the meaning of hope. How a person is present in a place and at a time greatly affects the meaning of both the place and the time. Wherever a person is he can take an attitude or a stance. This has a profound effect on the meaning of his presence. His attitude or stance determines the meaning of the place or the time. What does it mean to be at Harvard? That depends on the individual student. What does it mean to be present in a church? That depends on the individual worshiper. What does it mean to be a twenty-year old or an eighty-year old? That depends to a large extent on the person who is twenty or the person who is eighty. What does it mean to live during the twentieth century? That depends on how the person relates to radios, television, automobiles, and planes. *How* you are present is the key to what meanings are important to you and what meanings are irrelevant to you.

Being a person means putting your presence somewhere at some time in some manner. A person pays for the worlds he chooses. Personal living involves a risk. A person's radical response to his temporal-spatial situation determines who the person will be. Hope is such a response.

I "Make" My World

Using myself as an example may clarify some points about personal presence. There is a "Lauder-World." It is the world or worlds in which I live, that set of meanings that interest me and are real to me. The "Lauder-World" is a flexible world in the sense that it is either expanding or shrinking. The "Lauder-World" has come about through many influences. It is due to my parents and sister, to the people I've met, the schools I've attended, the books I've read, the films I've seen and hundreds of other contributing factors. My world changes every day as I open or close my self to new experiences. At times my world changes dramatically. When someone I love dies, my world seems shattered. When a new friend relates deeply to me, my world takes on a new brightness. A creative presence has entered it. When I'm lonely, my world seems dull and drab; when I'm loved my world seems beautiful and hope-filled.

I don't wish to give the impression that the "Lauder-World" comes about automatically or mechanically. While my world has been influenced by many factors, as a totality it is not determined. It is not some necessary product of a necessary cause. I believe that to a great extent it is due to my freedom. I choose my world. I choose the values to which I am committed. This is true of everyone. The world a person lives in is, at least to some extent, a world he has chosen.

If I live in a world which seems like a fantasy world, one in which the problems of people and of life are not disturbing to me, this is probably due to the fact that I have not allowed myself to grow up. Perhaps my friends have not encouraged me to grow up or have shielded me. To refuse to mature is to settle for a world that is narrow and shallow. In order for such a world to expand, the person may have to endure a great deal of pain and suffering. If it opens the person to the real needs around him, the pain will be justified. The person will grow up. Children are delightful, but usually only adults can help others. To be of service, some independence and maturity are necessary qualities. If a person moves from a fantasy world to a world in which other people's problems call to him for help, that person's world expands.

Hope is a way of being present to God. It is a way of standing before God with trust and confidence. Hope says "In spite of everything. . . ." No matter what the evidence seems to say, hope says that God is a Father who never forgets. Without hope, Christian charity cannot be present and Christian faith cannot direct the believer's life the way it should. Hope places us in a new world, a many-splendored world that puts our best dreams to shame.

Trust in God's Presence

The person who hopes in God risks everything on God's presence and promises. A person can be present in many ways. Hope puts the person on an existential tightrope: while he is walking it, he's trusting that he is in the hands of God. Hope is a gift from God, but it must be accepted by the person. God will not force hope upon us. Even God can't force us to hope. Essential to hope is that it be free. We are responsible for our hope. God's grace is necessary for hope but how we respond to that grace makes us responsible for our hope.

Presumption and despair are two ways of being present that are quite different from hope, yet they can illuminate the meaning of hope. The presumptuous person thinks that he is completely in charge of his life, the center of his world and totally in charge of his destiny. It is difficult to imagine how any adult except perhaps the least reflective can be presumptuous. You don't have to live very long, you don't have to experience more than one tragedy to realize that you are not the complete master of your future or the futures of those you love. Human experience is a tough teacher and the presumptuous person is a poor learner. I guess the presumptuous person's ego gets in the way of his vision.

The person who despairs goes to the opposite extreme. He has cut himself off from God's saving presence. He has forgotten that life is a gift and has severed himself from the presence of the gift-giver. For the despairing person life is hopeless. He knows he can't reach his goal alone, and he mistakenly thinks that he is alone. Despair is such a horrible sin because it distorts human presence and as far as possible converts human openness into "human closedness." It's a kind of spiritual suicide, a kind of direct attack on Love's Saving Self-Gift.

The meaning of hope is the confident placing of personal presence in the Presence of God. The person who hopes tries to use his talents and energies but knows that only God saves. Hope knows how to say "Abba, Father."

Hope Helps Us To See

Hope enables a person to unveil new meanings in his life. What scripture relates about Judas and Peter suggests that hope can unveil meanings not available to the person who refuses to hope. Apparently Judas despaired. Peter didn't. The vision of life held by these two apostles was completely different: one could see no reason to live, the other could see a reason not only to live but even to give his life away. By being hopefully present in the world we allow ourselves to see all sorts of meanings that otherwise would not be available to us. Two people can have lives that seem to the external observer to be quite similar, but the presence of hope in one and the absence of hope in the other means that they are present to God, to others, and to the world in radically different ways. One believes that reality is gracious and is ready to surrender himself. This changes his whole life. The person who hopes does everything differently from the person who doesn't. The person who hopes sees the past differently, the present differently, and the future differently. The person who hopes sees people differently. Hope puts a person at ease with God.

Both the meaning of hope and that hope can illuminate new meanings in a person's life are beautifully expressed in Charles Peguy's poem *Hope*. In the poem Peguy imagines God saying the following:

I am, says God, Master of the Three Virtues

Faith is a faithful wife.
Charity is an ardent mother.
But hope is a tiny girl.
. . . .
Faith is she who remains tense during centuries and
Charity is she who unbends during centuries and
    centuries.
But my little hope
is she who every morning
wishes us good day.
. . . .
Faith is she who watches during centuries and centuries.
Charity is she who watches during centuries and centuries.
But my little hope is she
who goes to bed every night
and gets up every morning
and really sleeps very well.

I am, says God, the Lord of that virtue.

My little hope is she
who goes to sleep every night,
in that child's crib of hers,
after having said her prayers properly,
and who every morning wakes up and rises
and says her prayers with a new look in her eyes.
. . . .
Faith is the sanctuary lamp
That burns forever.
Charity is that big, beautiful log fire
That you light in your hearth
So that my children the poor may come and warm
    themselves before it on winter evenings.

And all around Faith, I see all my faithful
Kneeling together in the same attitude, and with one voice
Uttering the same prayer.
And around Charity, I see all my poor
Sitting in a circle around that fire
And holding out their palms to the heat of the hearth.
But my hope is the bloom, and the fruit, and the leaf, and
  the limb,
And the twig, and the shoot, and the seed, and the bud.
Hope is the shoot, and the bud of the bloom
Of eternity itself.

Hope is essential to personal existence. It's our way of
responding to God's promise. It is the shoot, and the bud
of the bloom of eternity itself.

3 Hope: A Healing Presence

The Experience of Anxiety

Our age has frequently been described as an age of anxiety. Many seem to have to narcotize themselves with either alcohol or drugs just to be able to face the ordinary trials, stresses, and difficulties of everyday living. In his book *Man's Search for Himself*, psychologist Rollo May provides a good example to describe what anxiety is. May suggests that if you are walking along a highway and see a car speeding toward you, your heart beats more rapidly, you quickly measure the distance between yourself and the car and also how far you have to move to get to a safe area. Then as quickly as you can you move to that area. However, May points out that if, when you start to hurry across the road toward the safe area you see cars coming at you from the opposite direction, you suddenly are caught not knowing which way to turn. In contrast to the original feeling of fear you may now feel panicky and your vision may even begin to blur. Perhaps you have an impulse to run blindly in any direction. May says that after the cars have passed you may be aware of a slight faintness and a feeling of hollowness in the pit of your stomach. This, says May, is anxiety. May writes:

> In fear we know what threatens us, we are energized
> by the situation, our perceptions are sharper, and we

take steps to run or . . . other appropriate ways to overcome the danger. In anxiety, however, we are threatened without knowing what steps to take to meet the danger. Anxiety is the feeling of being "caught," "overwhelmed," and instead of becoming sharper, our perceptions generally become blurred or vague.

I went through a terrible experience of anxiety for many months when I was a seminarian, studying to be a priest. The memory of it is still vivid in my mind. I had an attack of scruples, a crippling anxiety about imagined sins that I had committed and was committing. Anyone who has had even the briefest bout with scruples knows how devastating they can be. Perhaps the saddest aspect of scrupulosity is that the person who suffers from it wants to grow closer to God but the scruples so turn him in on himself that while scrupulous he can't be a free mature person, able to develop a healthy relationship with his Father. The word "scruple" comes from the Latin word for "pebble" and the origin of the word tells us a great deal about the scrupulous person: on his journey toward God, instead of focusing on the loving Father who is calling him he is preoccupied with pebbles in his shoe. He can't put attention to what is really important about life and relationship with God because he has allowed his anxiety to rule him.

A Battle With Scruples

My own particular bout with scruples so tied me in knots that I marvel now that I was able to continue the daily routine of study at the seminary. The scruples became particularly bad as the academic year drew to a close. I could get no peace though I spoke to a number of priests about it. Each priest gave good advice: stop worrying, place your trust in God, these are foolish scruples you are having. I could hear the words and understand the meaning, but somehow I couldn't make the meaning my own. At times as a priest was telling me not to worry I was already worried that he had not correctly understood my motivation or that I had not accurately described what I was experiencing to him.

My problem seemed hopeless. As the academic year came to a close I think now that I was close to a breakdown, though I didn't realize it at the time. I had been seeking help but really had made it nearly impossible for anyone to help me. When the academic year ended and I went home for the summer vacation, I sought out the priest who had been my spiritual director when I was in college. I believed if anyone could help me he could. Throughout my years of preparation for the priesthood this man had been for me a kind of model of what a priest should be. He was profoundly human but a real believer. When he taught me in college he had opened new worlds for me— challenged me, excited me, inspired me. He was easily the best teacher I had had up to that time. I also thought he was the best priest I had ever known. Because in those days students never left the major seminary except for vacations I could not seek help from this priest until the summer vacation began. By the time the vacation arrived I was in pretty bad shape having gone through a really bad period in the last weeks of the academic year.

Writing this now I can clearly recall the first meeting the priest and I had on that June day more than twenty years ago. I had called him and told him that I had to see him about something very important. When we met I told the whole painful story. I don't think I described my situation as scrupulosity because I didn't have sufficient insight into it to give it that label. As I told my story, my priest friend never interrupted. After I finished my story, he did not offer any quick solutions or easy advice. He said that he had little to say at this moment, that he wanted some time to think about what I had told him. This surprised me. Maybe it surprised me because I thought he knew the answers to everything and would quickly solve my problems. Though I was surprised I was also encouraged. He saw the problem as serious and wanted time to figure out a course of action. He did say however that if I wasn't able to get the problem under control I shouldn't go on to the priesthood. Tied up in knots myself, I wouldn't be able to help anyone else. He also said, and this proved true, that if I came through the problem and went on to be a priest the experience of scrupulosity would help me to understand others and help them.

Over that summer we met regularly. Slowly he tried to lead me to trust and confidently hope in God's love. Through his priestly presence he healed me, relieved my anxiety and helped me to become free. I don't know whether the advice he gave me was very different from what I had heard from other priests, but because he was special in my life the advice took on a new weight and importance and I was able to hear what I had previously been unable to hear. What previously had not registered with me began to make a great deal of sense. One statement my friend made impressed me very much. Trying to help me see that God is a father not a tyrant he said "Bob, I am not at all afraid to die. Not because I have lived such an exemplary life but because of the mercy of God. I have complete trust in God's mercy." Somehow my friend's trust rubbed off on me. His hope called me to wholeness.

Finding a Meaning in Life

What happened between my priest friend and me can be explained to some extent psychologically. Existential therapists such as Rollo May and Victor Frankl stress that within a human person there are resources to transcend anxiety and to find meaning in life that will sustain a person. Both thinkers stress the mystery of human nature and the capacity of people to transcend difficulties. Certainly for both one of the keys to health is finding a meaning that will make your life worthwhile. I wonder if anything is as ` harmful to personal existence as lack of meaning. Rollo May wrote:

> It may sound surprising when I say, that on the basis of my own clinical practice as well as that of my psychological and psychiatric colleagues, that the chief problem of people in the middle decade of the twentieth century is *emptiness*. By that I mean not only that many people do not know what they want, they often do not have any clear idea of what they feel. When they talk about lack of autonomy, or lament their inability to make decisions—difficulties which are present in all decades—it soon becomes evident that their underlying problem is that they have no definite experience of their own desires or wants. Thus they feel swayed this way and that, with painful feelings of powerlessness, because they feel vacuous, empty. The complaint which leads them to come for help may be, for example, that their love relationships always break up or that they cannot go through with marriage plans or are dissatisfied with the marriage partner. But they do not talk long before they make it clear that they expect the marriage partner, real or hoped-for, to fill some lack, some vacancy within themselves, and they are anxious and angry because he or she doesn't.

Psychiatrist Victor Frankl bases his therapeutic approach on what he calls logotherapy. Believing that the will to meaning is a primary force in a person's life, Frankl in therapy tries to widen and broaden the patient's vision until the patient commits himself to a meaning or meanings that enable him to live a healthy human existence. Frankl stresses human responsibility. In *Man's Search for Meaning* (pp. 112–113) he wrote:

> By declaring that man is a responsible creature and must actualize the potential meaning of his life, I wish to stress that the true meaning of life is to be found in the world rather than within man or his own psyche, as though it was a closed system. By the same token, the real aim of human existence cannot be found in what is called self-actualization. Human existence is essentially self-transcendence rather than self-actualization. Self-actualization is not a possible aim at all, for the simple reason that the more a man would strive for it, the more he would miss it. For only to the extent to which man commits himself to the fulfillment of his life's meaning, to this extent he also actualizes himself. In other words, self-actualization cannot be attained if it is made an end in itself, but only as a side-effect of self-transcendence.

Hopeful Presence Heals

The view of personal existence that May and Frankl embrace is quite consonant with the view that I outlined in the first chapter, with the exception that as therapists they would not deal directly with God as specifically religious meaning. If we wish to use May's and Frankl's approach to counseling and therapy to explain what happened between me and my priest friend that led me out of my anxiety and scruples, it would be that through his hopeful presence he healed me. Through his hopeful presence he enabled me to affirm new meaning in my life. It's important to note that he did not give me new information. In the usual meaning of the word knowledge, I *knew* everything that he told me about God's goodness and about how I should trust in his loving providence. However, the knowledge wasn't real to me, it was not really *my* meaning. I had not freely affirmed it in any decisive way in my life nor allowed it to play any important role in my life. Though his hope affected me, *I* had to hope. He couldn't do it for me. Sooner or later each of us is alone in a dark room with God. Each of us is responsible for what happens in that room. By hoping I was healed.

In *Love and Will* Rollo May stresses that what the therapist has to do is help the patient form a new intentionality. The technical word *intentionality* has an important meaning. It means a person's life stance or ultimate interpretation of reality. It might be described as a person's faith or outlook on life. May believes, and Frankl would agree, that when a patient has some psychological or emotional problem there is something lacking in his intentionality. In *The Unconscious God: Psychotherapy and Theology*, Frankl even argues that an excessively narrow view of reality, which he judges the atheistic view to be, can be harmful in terms of a person's psychological and emotional health. Intentionality goes beyond a person's intentions. It is a pervasive attitude toward life. May points out, "Intentionality is what underlies both conscious and unconscious intentions. It refers to a state of being and involves, to a greater or lesser degree, the *totality* of the person's orientation to the world at that time." Because it involves the totality of the person's orientation intentionality always involves a commitment. May claims that the degree of one's intentionality depends on the degree of one's courage. I would want to say that it depends on the degree of one's hope.

To see the role of hope in human living, not just psychological and emotional health must be considered but the meaning and direction of personal existence must be examined. Not only in my experience of anxiety when I suffered from severe scruples but in all types of anxiety—anxiety about death, about a successful marriage, about a choice of career—hope is the crucial element. Hope opens us to new meanings and to a new world. Hope gives us a taste of our final home. Hope can help us conquer not only psychological anxiety but also what might be called "ontological anxiety"—the anxiety that arises not because of some psychological problem but because of human freedom's search for a goal that will fulfill the deepest needs of the human heart. There is a dynamic relation between a person's presence and his world, between a person and the network of meanings that are real to him. A person's hopeful presence ought to continually open his world, extend it, and broaden it. Hope ought to make him more alive, more dynamically present. Hope ought to make a person whole. Isn't it our experience that the most interested people are also the most interesting? Isn't it our experience that people who are bored with everything are also boring? Reality is interesting and exciting for persons who open themselves to it. Two persons can have what seems to be the same experience and yet their interpretation and reaction to it are completely different. This could be due to their different visions of reality. To the man who believes that reality is absurd, suffering is complete tragedy.

To the man who believes that reality is meaningful, who hopes that reality is ultimately gracious, suffering may be a call to a new "world."

Hope and the Human Body

Any meditation on the mystery of person or on the virtue of hope should focus on the meaning of the human body. Hope is tied to the human body. In exploring how hope deepens personal existence, we are interested in the human body precisely insofar as it is human, that is, insofar as it participates in personhood. It is the only body of its kind within our experience. Though the bodies of some animals bear superficial resemblances to the human body, as far as we can determine there is more dissimilar than similar between an animal's body and a human body. The reason for this is that the human body shares in personhood. Whether you think of the body as somehow participating in your person or as a thing you carry around with you has important implications for your outlook on just about every aspect of human living. An obvious area that would be affected is your view of sexuality. Is being sexual a way of being a thing or a way of being a person?

Some sense of the radical responsibility that a person has for his existence begins to dawn when we consider the mystery of bodily presence. Human bodiliness has to be somewhere. How, when, and where it is present greatly affects the person. I am responsible for my bodiliness. It is my way of being in worlds. Hope is a way of being bodily present, a way of being in a world. This way of being bodily present that we call hope opens us to new meanings.

Many of us have thought of knowing as a kind of blotter

experience. May's notion of intentionality can correct that. We may have overlooked or forgotten the active part a person plays in knowing anything. We have thought of meaning as lying around waiting to be easily picked up by the mind. Some meanings are easily picked up, some are not. Every meaning requires a particular stance, a particular angle of vision, a particular perspective, a particular gift of self. Science requires one angle of vision, poetry another, religion another. To read a poem as though it were a science manual is to miss the meaning of the poem completely; to try to study religious meaning from the angle of a scientist is to make it impossible for the religious meaning to break through to your consciousness. You are bound to miss the point because you haven't assumed the angle of vision or the perspective required in order to grasp the meaning that is presented. I am not saying that you must agree with the religious meaning that is presented, but you must open your consciousness to religious meaning, you must take a particular stance, assume a particular perspective so that you can perceive the religious meaning.

In any discussion you must know the angle, perspective, or stance that the other person is taking. The first step toward answering any question is to make sure that you understand the meaning of the question. Only when you know the angle of vision from which the questioner is speaking can you hope to meet him where he is. Only when you know the stance from which the questioner is speaking can you hope to grasp and respond to his question. If you speak from another angle or another stance you may be providing an answer to some question but not to the question he is asking. All meaning depends on the angle of vision of the viewer, on the presence of the person, on the particular stance that the person takes.

As an example to illustrate the importance of intentionality, let us consider the meaning of death. Any person knows that he is going to die. However, a doctor, a funeral director, and a person who has just learned that he has a terminal disease will take three different stances on death. The doctor looks at death medically, the funeral director looks at death as part of his business, and the dying person from the most radical and personal point of view. The three persons are focusing on three different meanings of death. The dying person is searching for the ultimate meaning. The meaning he comes up with will be intimately related to how he answers the question "Who am I?" It will be related to his basic stance on life or his angle of vision toward reality. It will be related to his hope or lack of hope.

Hope: Stance Toward Reality

The basic stance that a person takes toward reality is related to, though not identical with, his wishes and desires. Every person has a radical stance in relation to the meaning of reality. A person's stance both feeds and is fed by the person's plans, projects, and intentions. My angle of vision is how and where I stand in relation to what is other than me. It's how I perceive reality. How a person perceives reality nourishes and encourages a person's dreams, wishes, and intentions and, in turn, these structure and strengthen his stance. If a person believes that love is the most meaningful human activity, then this will direct that person's intentions, plans, and projects. Such a person's intentions and wishes concerning love will also open up and reveal new meanings and deeper meanings to the person as he views reality. The person's intentions will affect his basic vision of life. He can be hopeful. On the other hand, a person who does not believe that love is the most meaningful human activity will have a different outlook, a different view of reality, and also will have different wishes, plans, and projects. He may be courting despair.

Hope is a way of being bodily present in the world and it participates in a person's basic intentionality, his basic interpretation and vision of reality. The ultimate intentionality of a Christian believer would be his faith—his belief that God is a Father, that personal existence has a purpose, that there is life beyond death. Hope shares and supports that vision. What is faith like for the person who has lost hope? It's difficult to imagine. Though he might affirm Christian meanings such as the fatherhood and providence of God, the resurrection of the dead, and the eucharist, how real could those meanings be to him? They would be lifeless meanings for him because he lacked hope.

Hope changes a person's relationship to God and to the rest of the world. This is why it's important to stress that hope is a way of being bodily present. We wish to avoid all traces of "angelism"—all temptations to treat a person as a disembodied spirit who through hope can focus on some spiritual world and disregard the world in which the rest of the human race is struggling and suffering. A human person is bodied and hope is encountered in the fleshly reality that a person is. Hope can affect the way a person walks, talks, eats; whether he sings or dances, whether he feels good or bad about himself. Hope should deeply affect what he decides to do with his life and how he relates to others.

The vision of personal existence that May and Frankl affirm is fine if psychological health is being discussed. If the deepest needs of the human heart are being discussed, then the virtue of hope must enter the picture. Without it a person doesn't have a chance. People are made for God and he is the heart's hope. What happened between me and my spiritual director is a pale image of what should happen between a person and God. My priest friend's hopeful presence healed me and called me to hope. God through his presence calls us all to hope. Through scruples and anxiety I was turned in on myself and unable to move creatively into the future. Without God's self-giving presence we would be hopelessly turned in on ourselves. I guess we'd be in hell. Hell is home for the hopeless.

Two Dramas Shed Light on Hope

I suppose the first step toward hope is to realize our helplessness without God. While our secular culture befogs many other important religious meanings there are some signs that it may help some people toward the "ontological anxiety" which may highlight the need for hope. Two recent award-winning plays raise important questions to which I believe hope is the answer.

Michael Cristoffer's Pulitzer Prize-winning *The Shadow Box* takes place in three cottages on the grounds of a large hospital. The cottages are for terminally ill patients and their families. At the hosptial there is a special program to help both the ill person and that person's family. The general idea of the program, as far as I can make out, is to help people face the reality of death.

A number of things were interesting about the play. First, although it might sound morbid, the topic of the play was interesting. I believe that the best way to have a full meaningful life is to confront the reality of death. This doesn't mean becoming preoccupied with death and fixating on the fact of death; it does involve asking what human life means in the face of death. Over the years I have thought a great deal about death and I have come to believe that if death were the end of the human person then human life would be absurd. There are people who do not believe in any personal existence beyond death and yet find fulfillment and meaning in their lives. They believe that in spite of death being the end of personal existence a person can find sufficient meaning to make his or her life worthwhile. I think they are wrong. I believe that if death is the end then life is absurd. My view of death does not force me to minimize the importance of this life; rather it helps me to see the beauty of personal existence—even death can't destroy it.

Another interesting aspect of the play was the diversity of character in the three terminally ill patients. The playwright, Michael Cristoffer, wanted to make the point strongly that death will come to everyone. There was no reference to immortality in the play. Whatever Cristoffer's personal belief, not mentioning immortality did have a powerful effect: the reality of death was dramatically highlighted. Beginning the play on a low key, Cristoffer builds to a crescendo as the reality of death is finally faced by all the characters in the play and I imagine by all the people in the theater. In trying to assure that every member of the audience confront the reality of death, Cristoffer has a powerful ending to his drama. All the characters face the audience. Each speaks briefly a number of times forming a kind of chorus and the overall effect is quite rhythmic, almost poetic. The lines that are spoken at the audience pick up in speed and in dramatic power. A number of the characters say "yes." I suppose this is their acceptance of their death. It's probably also meant to be their affirmation of life. Perhaps it is also Cristoffer's affirmation of life. But what are they affirming? If death is the end, to what are the characters saying "yes"? The reality of death? The reality of life? The beauty of life? But is life beautiful if death is the end? Is there any hope if death is the end? I don't think so. Hope is possible precisely because the truth about ourselves is that death isn't the end.

The plot of Peter Shaffer's *Equus* concerns a teenage boy who for some mysterious reason gouges out the eyes of some horses. A psychiatrist tries to solve the mystery while helping the young man to become normal. Most of the play centers around the sessions between the psychiatrist, who is struggling with the meaning of his own life, and the young boy who, prior to his crime, had a passionate love of horses. What is most interesting about *Equus* is the general question that the play poses through the psychiatrist's self-questioning. Viewing contemporary persons as "hollow men," as passionless, uncommitted creatures, and including himself among their number, the psychiatrist wonders what cause or what person is worthy of a passionate commitment. In effect, the psychiatrist asks, "What, if anything, can contemporary man worship?"

It may be unusual for a contemporary playwright like Peter Shaffer to ask questions about worship. But what shouldn't be forgotten is that religious questions are inevitable in life. Eventually, everyone must opt for some interpretation of reality. No one can escape ultimate questions. "Who am I?" "What's the meaning of life?" "To what or to whom do I wish to give myself?" are questions that confront everyone. They are religious questions in the sense that they deal with a person's basic life stance. They do not deal with institutional religion; they are religious in a more basic sense. In this sense, everyone is religious. The atheist, the agnostic, the Communist, and the Christian are religious. Each has taken a basic stance toward the meaning of reality. Even the person whose attitude is "I don't want to be bothered with ultimate questions" has a religion. Because every person is religious, every person is a believer. There is no avoiding belief. The question is what should a person believe in? That's the question that *Equus* raises, and that's why it is such a fascinating play.

At the end of *Equus* the psychiatrist has decided to cure the teenage boy even though it means that the lad will lose his passion for life. The psychiatrist, jealous of the boy's passion and commitment, feels that his own life is empty. Saddened by the lack of purpose in his life but also wondering if human existence has some ultimate meaning, the psychiatrist feels that the experience of counseling the teenager has raised unavoidable questions in his own mind. The last words of the play are spoken by the psychiatrist to the audience

> And now for me it never stops: that voice of Equus out of the cave—"Why Me? . . . Why Me? . . . Account for Me." . . . .All right—I surrender! I say it! . . . In an ultimate sense I cannot know what I do in this place—yet I do ultimate things. Essentially I cannot know what I do—yet I do essential things. Irreversible, terminal things. I stand in the dark with a pick in my hand, striking at heads! I need—more desperately than my chil-

dren need me—a way of seeing in the dark. What way is this? . . . *What dark is this?* . . . I cannot call it ordained of God: I can't get that far. I will however pay it so much homage. There is now, in my mouth, this sharp chain. And it never comes out.

Hope is a way of seeing in the dark.

"Ontological anxiety" ought to be normal and natural for persons who reflect on their experience. It's a tragedy if a society or a culture crush the "ontological anxiety" of people rather than support and encourage their struggle to face it and if possible find some hope. Fortunately for all of us God has given us reason to hope. Our God is a God of presence and promise. Because he is, we can hope and be healed.

4 Hope and God's Promise

Human persons are creatures who live through meaning. For human growth and development, meaning is crucial. Through the meanings in his life, through the meanings that are real to him an individual develops or declines in terms of the richness of personal existence. If a person is to achieve the promise that is his, images and symbols of hope are required to nourish him, to help him move creatively into the future. For the Christian the images of hope that are essential for his Christian existence are the images provided by God in salvation history.

Abraham as Father of Hope

Abraham is called the father of faith but he might also be called the father of hope. In his story we have all the elements of the experience of hope: a confusing and frightening trap that seems to offer no way out and then a new freedom is achieved through hope. Abraham is called by God to leave his familiar surroundings and go into an unknown land. Anyone who has had the experience of leaving the known and journeying into the unknown appreciates how frightening that experience can be. It's very much like entering a dark room. The only light that Abraham has is the word of God. Receptive to that word he journeys forth. His hope is tested when God, who has promised Abraham that he will be the father of a great nation, asks Abraham to take his only son Isaac and slay him. We have heard the story so frequently that we can overlook the tension and confusion that Abraham must have felt. How could he be the father of a great nation when God was asking him to sacrifice his only son? Though the details of Abraham's trial will probably never be duplicated, every Christian who is at all sensitive to suffering, tragedy, and evil, is in a situation similar to Abraham's. The Christian may not be asked by God to take his son to a high mountain for slaughter, but at times he will be called into a dark room that will be the same existential experience that Abraham had. How can the problem be solved? How can the light dawn? Is all hopeless? Is all lost? Abraham heard God's word and placed his trust in God. Because of Abraham's trust, God rescinded the order to slay Isaac. Christians believe that by trusting in their Father no situation can crush them. They may not see the light, they may not feel the consolation, but they believe and hope that God, who is a loving Father is present and that he will keep his promises just as he kept his promise to Abraham who became the father of a great nation, the Jewish people.

God Makes Promises

The call that was made to Abraham is repeated to other leaders of the Jewish people as the story of this special people develops. An especially important call is made to Moses who is to lead the people in the Exodus journey. If we read the story of the Jewish people with the eyes of faith, a repeated and continuing pattern can be discerned: God makes himself present to his people. This presence itself is a kind of promise and always contains the promise of continued presence. In the Exodus experience, after Moses has led the people out of Egypt, God makes a covenant with his people. As events succeed one another in Old Testament history the nature of this covenant becomes more clear to the Jewish people. At times it is expressed in rather material and physical terms. But right from the beginning it was clear that the covenant was between God and a people. The community believed that God was specially present to them and had made promises to them as a people. It is not just that an individual Jew hoped in God, but a people hoped in God for their fulfillment as a community. These people could hope because God had promised that he would always be present to them, and his very continuing presence was the beginning of the fulfillment of his promise. The deepest insight into God's presence and promise had to wait until the coming of Jesus. In this man God's presence was a fulfillment of God's promise and was also the hope for the completion of God's promise in a future kingdom. As the relationship between the Jewish people and God developed, the promise of God to his people became located in the awaited coming of a Messiah. However, the nature of the Messiah and of the kingdom was not grasped until God spoke his ultimate Word in Jesus. This is why even some of those who eagerly hoped for the fulfillment of God's promise in the Messiah did not recognize the Messiah when he came.

Hope and the Coming of Jesus

New with the coming of Jesus is the clear hope in the resurrection of the body. With Jesus' coming and resurrection, hope takes on a new incarnation: it is deeply rooted in history because of the earthly life of Jesus but also looks beyond history to a richer union with God because of Jesus' resurrection. Now God is present to his people in a special way because of the presence of his risen Son in the midst of the Christian community. Because of the risen Lord's presence, the Christian is hoping for his own personal fulfillment but also for the fulfillment of the community. Both will happen, he hopes, when the kingdom of God arrives in its fullness.

Between the past deeds that God has performed in Christ and the future coming of the kingdom in its fullness the role of the Holy Spirit is central to the life of the Christian and to the growth of the Christian community. The Spirit is an animating spirit of hope. St. Paul says "May the God of hope bring you such joy and peace in your faith that the power of the Holy Spirit will remove all bounds to hope" (Rom 15: 13).

The fullness of hope is beautifully if somewhat obscurely depicted in the Book of Revelation. Though details of the future kingdom are not clearly stated and much of the book requires careful interpretation, what is crystal clear is that the Christian should have complete and utter confidence in the fulfillment of God's promises and that this fulfillment will be the special presence of God to his people, the intimate love and friendship that will be established. "Then I heard a loud voice call from the throne, 'You see this city? Here God lives among men. He will make his home among them; they shall be his people, and he will be their God; his name is God-with-them. He will wipe away all tears from their eyes; there will be no more death, and no more mourning or sadness. The world of the past has gone'" (Rev 21: 3-4).

Paul: Apostle of Hope

There are so many stirring references to hope in St. Paul that he might well be called the apostle of hope. What seems unique about St. Paul is that for him hope can reach out not only to include all persons but even to include creation itself.

I think that what we suffer in this life can never be compared to the glory, as yet unrevealed, which is waiting for us. The whole creation is eagerly waiting for God to reveal his sons. It was not for any fault on the part of creation that it was made unable to attain its purpose, it was made so by God; but creation still retains the hope of being freed, like us, from its slavery to decadence, to enjoy the same freedom and glory as the children of God. From the beginning till now the entire creation, as we know, has been groaning in one great act of giving birth; and not only creation, but all of us who possess the first fruits of the Spirit, we too groan inwardly as we wait for our bodies to be set free (Romans 8: 18-23).

Commentators have pointed out that St. Paul urges us to be daring in our hope, confident that God will not let us down. St. Paul seems to suggest that the very difficulties of our life should lead us to hope more passionately.

So far then we have seen that, through our Lord Jesus Christ, by faith we are judged righteous and at peace with God, since it is by faith and through Jesus that we have entered this state of grace in which we can boast about looking forward to God's glory. But that is not all we can boast about; we can boast about our sufferings. These sufferings bring patience, as we know, and patience brings perseverance, and perseverance brings hope, and this hope is not deceptive, because the love of God has been poured into our hearts by the Holy Spirit which has been given us (Romans 5: 1-5).

For St. Paul hope is the anchor offered us through Christ the high priest. God will keep his promises.

When God made the promise to Abraham, he swore by his own self, since it was impossible for him to swear by anyone greater: I will shower blessings on you and give you many descendants. Because of that, Abraham persevered and saw the promise fulfilled. Men, of course, swear an oath by something greater than themselves, and between men, confirmation by an oath puts an end to all dispute. In the same way, when God wanted to make the heirs to the promise thoroughly realize that his purpose was unalterable, he conveyed this by an oath; so that there would be two unalterable things in which it was impossible for God to be lying, and so that we, now we have found safety, should have a strong encouragement to take a firm grip on the hope that is held out to us. Here we have an anchor for our soul, as sure as it is firm, and reaching right through beyond the veil where Jesus has entered before us and on our behalf, to become a high priest of the order of Melchizedek, and for ever (Hebrews 6: 13-20).

Hope is an anchor that is especially helpful in the storm of life. The Christian is not confined to the scriptures for encouragements to hope. The sacraments surround his earthly existence, and every sacrament is a pledge and a promise of God's faithfulness. Sacraments are signs of hope and signs to deepen our hope. Any sacrament could be analyzed from the point of view of hope. Recently I attended an ordination to holy orders and the entire ceremony spoke of hope.

Priestly Ordination: A Sign of Hope

There may be no event that so calls attention to the mystery and meaning of our faith as the ordination of a minister of the gospel. The ordination I attended was of a young man whom I taught when he was a college seminarian. The ordination ceremony was inspiring, and it said something important about the meaning of ministry. What came through clearly in the ceremony was that a minister of the gospel is a man taken from the community and ordained so that he can serve the community. Every aspect of the ordination ceremony spoke that loudly and clearly. It also spoke of the young man's hope and the Christian community's hope.

At the ordination the parish teenage choir sang beautifully. Many of those teenagers had come to know and love the young man and their pride and joy was evident by their presence and singing. There was a sense of pride and joy throughout the congregation: the organist, the director of song, the servers, the young man's family and friends, the hundreds of parishioners all revealed it. In some special way the newly ordained was their minister.

Their presence at the ceremony was a hope-filled presence.

During the ordination ceremony my mind went back five or six years to when I had taught the young man. I remembered classes he attended, the projects we tackled together, discussions we had. I realized how much he had grown in five years. I mused a bit on what his experience of ministry might be. I thought back on my own experience of the last seventeen years, years in which I had been surrounded by God's goodness and generosity, and I wondered what the future held for the new levite.

In the booklet designed by the young man and given out at the ceremony there was a quotation from Thomas Merton that captures the mystery of the day, the mystery of Christian living, and the mystery of hope.

> My Lord God, I have no idea where I am going, I do not see the road ahead of me. I cannot know for certain where it will end. Nor do I really know myself, and the fact that I think that I am following your will does not mean that I am actually doing so. But I believe that the desire to please you does in fact please you. And I hope that I will never do anything apart from what you desire. And I know that if I do this you will lead me by the right road though I may know nothing about it. Therefore, I will trust you always though I may seem to be lost and in the shadow of death. I will not fear, for you are ever with me and you will never leave me to face my perils alone.

Each of us could pray that prayer and mean it. No one knows what lies in the future. But we believe that the future will be colored by God's love. There may be no event that so calls attention to the mystery and meaning of our faith as the ordination of a minister of the gospel. The entire ceremony speaks of hope.

Hope and the Christian Storyteller

Besides scripture and sacraments the Christian looks for signs of hope in his daily living. In our society the media do not support Christian hope. It is for this reason that the Christian storyteller is of particular importance. In a special way the Christian storyteller can feed our hope.

Listening to or reading stories with a Christian dimension can be inspiring. Anyone who professes the Christian faith believes that the most accurate depiction of reality is provided by Christian revelation. A storyteller who introduces that dimension is writing about the way things really are. He is holding the mirror up to reality. His vision of faith does not excuse him from being a good writer but it can focus in important ways whatever talent he might have. The Christian storyteller has a marvelous vocation.

Every person writes his own story. By his free choice he creates himself and his future. The ultimate meaning of a person's life is the meaning he has chosen. What a person thinks of himself, what a person accepts as his self-image, what he accepts as an interpretation of reality, feed in to help him write his story. A person writes his story by the free choices that he makes.

Christians don't believe that human persons are the only authors of their stories. God co-authors every story. The story of Jesus intertwines with the story of every other person. The Christ-event—the birth, death, resurrection, ascension of Jesus—colors every other human story. Jesus' story reveals the meaning of reality. Only by tying his own story into the story of Jesus can a person hope to experience life in its richest and most profound dimensions.

The Christian storyteller knows this, and by telling certain types of stories the Christian storyteller can remind the rest of us. What kind of stories? That's not easy to say. Even the expression "Christian storyteller" is not easy to explain. Certainly a Christian storyteller is not someone who just happens to be a Christian. Nor are Christian stories those which happen to be populated by characters who are Christian. There is a more important dimension. I believe that a Christian story must somehow call attention to the mystery of Christ and the mystery of Christianity. The Christian storyteller may focus his attention on those realities either directly or indirectly, either explicitly or implicitly.

The vocation of the Christian storyteller is magnificent, but it is a vocation not easy to fulfill. In trying to write a story with a Christian dimension, it is easy for the author to reduce the tale to a pious sermon. Instead of a story what is read is more like a homily or pious exhortation. The Christian storyteller must recount real stories, about flesh and blood people in concrete situations. In holding the mirror up to the supernatural, the Christian storyteller must not neglect the natural settings, circumstances and scenes that are part of people's experience. The genius of the great Christian storyteller is to show life but to show it from the unique vision that is his as a Christian. No easy task, but when he is successful literature is produced that is both inspired and inspiring.

Recently I saw a performance of Graham Greene's *The Potting Shed* put on by the students at the college seminary where I teach, and I viewed it with genuine excitement. Whatever its dramatic merits—and I think they are many

— *The Potting Shed* spoke deeply to me. Greene tried to say something about the mystery of the resurrection. I think he succeeded but that a contemporary artist should even try I find very exciting. Late in the play the main character, James Callifer, who has come to believe that through a miracle his life has been restored to him, is trying to explain to his ex-wife Sara why he now loves her in a way that he couldn't when he believed that there was no point to human existence. Describing his previous love-less approach both to her and to life, Callifer says, "I'd no idea what love was in those days. I was the wrong man to make a deathbed marriage. Nothing mattered. If I slept with you, what did it matter? We were all going to be dead as last year's dog. Now, when I look at you, I see someone who will never die forever. Sara, you never believed I wanted you and you were right. Your kiss was always a question, and I hadn't got an answer. I couldn't love you any more than you can love a tree, a glass of wine, a cat."

Some people find this type of dialogue too academic—almost like an apologetics class, but I find it exciting. Why? I think it's because I so often feel starved when I encounter modern drama and film. I don't think I'm a philistine in evaluating contemporary drama and film. I find the viewpoints and world visions of writers and talented artists interesting and often provocative. Yet I often find their visions inadequate, wanting, even myopic. What they see, many portray better than I could ever hope to but what they see frequently seems to be a tiny portion of the human mystery. They don't call me to hope.

It was playwright Eugene O'Neill who said that all significant drama deals with the relationship between God and man. I'm sympathetic to O'Neill's view. As a Christian I believe the relationship between God and man is unequalled in importance. It has tremendous potential for drama. I also believe as a Christian that Christian revelation sheds the most important kind of light on the human mystery. Contemporary artists live in a post-Christian world. The atmosphere and climate of contemporary society does not encourage religious drama. Today's artists are not nourished by Christian symbols. Often the important artists have rejected their religious traditions. For many Christians hope is dead.

There is a more basic problem, one that is indigenous to religious drama. How can an artist concretize the mystery of God? How can a playwright or story writer incarnate the mystery of God on a stage or in a story? The poor track record of many who have tried is the best indication of how difficult the task is. Difficult as it is to create, religious drama has tremendous power to nourish and humanize us. Religious drama can help us to hope.

Today what Christian storytellers are people reading? One of the best is Flannery O'Connor. A Southern Catholic with a distinctly Christian view of life, the very talented Miss O'Connor suffered terribly from lupus disease before her death in 1964. A Christian storyteller, she wrote knowingly about the South, its traditions, beauty, and faults. Her stories replay similar themes. There is a contrast between the absurdity of the world which has as its source the sinfulness of people and the absurdity introduced by Christ, which is absurd in the sense that it is totally different from what most people believe about life or expect from it. Christ destroys the balance of things. A frequent theme in O'Connor's writing is that in order to find Christ you almost have to lose everything else. Christ comes in a special way through suffering. Through pain and loss our eyes are opened: we can see in a new way. It's as though our comfortable position in the world has blinded us. It has clouded our hope.

A number of O'Connor's stories could be used to illustrate the central place Christian hope had in her vision. I think it's fair to say that her story, *A Displaced Person,* is about Christian hope. The displaced person is a refugee from war-torn Poland who, through a priest, gets a job on a Southern plantation. At first the owner, a Mrs. McIntire, likes him very much because he works so hard. However, when she finds his views of black people are different from her own she wants to get rid of him. Every time she tries to tell the priest, he uses the opportunity to instruct her in the faith. Insisting that she is not interested in Christianity and that Christ was just another displaced person, Mrs. McIntire claims that she is interested in more important things like running her plantation. Throughout the story a beautiful peacock spreads its multi-colored wings. The priest says, "Christ will come like that." As the priest looks at the peacock, Mrs. McIntire, speaking of the workman, asks, "Why did he come anyway?" Speaking of Christ, Fr. Flynn says, "He came to redeem us."

Near the end of the story, a jealous co-worker allows a fatal accident to happen to the displaced person. Though she could have prevented it, Mrs. McIntire doesn't. This sin is her final downfall. Gradually she and the plantation begin to disintegrate. Struck with a nervous disease, Mrs. McIntire declines rapidly. When she becomes bedridden, Fr. Flynn is the only visitor she ever has. The following is the last sentence in the story: "He came regularly once a week with a bag of bread crumbs and after he had fed these to the peacock, he would come in and sit by the side of her bed and explain the doctrines of the Church."

The story is quite provocative. Flannery O'Connor raises

all sorts of questions about Christianity. Like all good Christian storytellers she calls our attention to the Good News in a way that reminds us that it really is news. It is easy for us to allow our Christianity to become routine. At times we need a jolt, a shock or a new insight in order to see God's gifts in a new way. The very strangeness of the priest in *The Displaced Person* calls attention to this. He seems to think Christ is more important than anything. Aren't all of us supposed to think this? To hope in Christ means that we realize that Christ is our only hope.

Today there are many factors working against the Christian storyteller's success. In an essay Flannery O'Connor wrote:

> The problem of the novelist who wishes to write about a man's encounter with this God is how he shall make the experience—which is both natural and supernatural—understandable, and credible, to his reader. In any age this would be a problem, but in our own, it is a well-nigh insurmountable one. Today's audience is one in which religious feeling has become, if not atrophied, at least vaporous and sentimental.

The Christian storyteller can make a great contribution to people. Christians are exhorted to allow their faith to color and effect all their actions. Often incarnating a Christian vision into day-to-day existence seems an impossible task. There are so few aids and supports. Christianity can be reduced to a Sunday affair. The Christian storyteller helps to prevent this from happening. He calls us to hope. He reminds us of God's promise and God's presence.

5 Hope and Human Wholeness

T. S. Eliot wrote, "Human kind cannot bear very much reality." It seems that the richness of reality is too much for us. Either we don't relate to God or we relate poorly. A faith relationship with God calls us to walk on a tightrope. Though we may occasionally do such walking we seem to be only too eager to step back onto the firm ground. Eliot said human kind cannot bear very much reality. We might add that it seems as though human kind cannot bear very much God. We seem to want to take God on our own terms. Of course this is really not to take him at all.

To be a person is to be in danger. To be a person is to be in a risky situation. To be a person is to be called to hope. We have no choice about whether we will or will not risk. Our choice is how we will risk, where we will take a chance. Will we walk the Christian tightrope? This is up to us. Though God calls us to it, he will never *make* us walk. Tightropes must be walked freely.

The Risk of Christian Living

A paradox related to Christian living is that by embracing the dangers of Christian living, we open ourselves to the deepest possible fulfillment. All persons take risks and all persons believe. To be a Christian is to be called to become like the person Jesus. It is to be called to deliver yourself to a Father and to risk everything on that Father's love. To be a Christian is not to play it safe. Rather it is to open yourself to the deepest dimensions of experience. To succeed is to reach the deepest dimensions of personal existence. It is to allow the promise within your person to be fulfilled.

The importance of taking risks if we're going to grow as persons is beautifully illustrated in what seems to be a children's story but is really a profoundly beautiful tale for all who have sufficient experience to catch its meaning. The story is Margery Williams' *The Velveteen Rabbit* (Doubleday, 1926 and 1958). The importance of risking ourselves and of gambling on other people's love for us is delightfully captured by the author.

The story concerns a toy, a velveteen rabbit, which occupies a neglected spot in a little boy's nursery. Finding life relatively unexciting and feeling neglected by its owner, the rabbit asks another toy, a skin horse, what *real* means. The skin horse has been loved by the little boy's uncle and because of that love has experienced a level of reality that is not accessible to the velveteen rabbit. With the wisdom of those who know what love can accomplish, the skin horse tries to explain the meaning of "real" to the rabbit:

> 'Real isn't how you are made,' said the Skin Horse. 'It's a thing that happens to you. When a child loves you for a long, long time, not just to play with, but REALLY loves you, then you become Real.'
> 'Does it hurt?' asked the Rabbit.
> 'Sometimes,' said the Skin Horse, for he was always truthful. 'When you are Real you don't mind being hurt.'

'Does it happen all at once, like being wound up,' he asked, 'or bit by bit?'

'It doesn't happen all at once,' said the Skin horse. 'You become Real. It takes a long time. That's why it doesn't often happen to people who break easily, or have sharp edges, or who have to be carefully kept!'

The skin horse knows that becoming real takes time and involves risk. He is telling the rabbit that in order to become real you have to open yourself, make yourself vulnerable. In terms of our discussion, what the skin horse is saying is that certain levels of living are only available to people who allow themselves to surrender to others, to gamble on the concern and love offered to them by others. Some levels of living are only open to those who hope in others.

No one finds gambling on the love or concern of others easy. It's like Abraham being called into a new land. Because we are uncertain of what is ahead of us, we are afraid. Similarly, because we are relying on the love offered by others, and because they may disappoint us, we are afraid to open ourselves, frightened of allowing ourselves to be opened.

When the velveteen rabbit thinks about what the skin horse has told him, he wants very much to be real, but he doesn't want to pay the price. He's afraid to hope. The risk and suffering that are demanded if someone is going to be real frighten him. Describing the velveteen rabbit, Margery Williams wrote, "He wished he could become it [Real] without those uncomfortable things happening to him." Like the velveteen rabbit we are afraid, yet somehow when we open ourselves to the loving concern of others we experience growth and freshness. In a special way, other persons can call us to a new level of personal existence. God calls us to hope in him because he wants to draw us into a perfect community, the community of Father, Son, and Spirit.

Promise Present Within Personal Existence

God has placed a promise within the meaning of person. It may be a promise that at times is difficult to discover and perhaps even more difficult to articulate when it is discovered. Nevertheless it is present. Unless it is recognized I doubt if our vision of person can have all the richness that it should have. Reflection on the meaning and mystery of person can reveal the promise within person. There are a number of ways of analyzing person so that the promise can be revealed. Some hint of the meaning of the promise can be seen by analyzing the mystery of personal presence. Even the insights into the meaning of personal presence by a contemporary atheist such as existentialist Albert Camus give some hint of the promise planted within person by God.

In his essay "The Myth of Sisyphus" Camus retells the Greek myth of Sisyphus. For refusing to return to the underworld Sisyphus was punished by the gods. Believing that they had thought up the perfect punishment to crush him, the gods condemn Sisyphus to pushing a rock up a hill for all eternity. To complete the frustration that the gods thought they had included in the punishment, each time the rock reached the top of the hill it would roll down again. When Sisyphus observed this and realized how hopeless this task was, he would experience, so the gods thought, total frustration. In relating the myth Camus emphasizes the return of Sisyphus down from the top of the hill. Camus sees that moment as the moment of truth. That is the moment in which light dawns. It is the moment when consciousness breaks through and overcomes the frustration. In Camus' universe it is the moment when person is most human. Camus writes:

> It is during that return, that pause, that Sisyphus interests me. A face that toils so close to stones is already stone itself. I see that man going back down with a heavy yet measured step toward the torment of which he will never know the end. That hour like a breathing-space which returns as surely as his suffering, that is the hour of consciousness. At each of those moments when he leaves the heights and gradually sinks toward the lairs of the gods, he is superior to his fate, he is stronger than his rock.

Why does Camus believe that Sisyphus is stronger than his rock? The answer lies in the nature of personal presence. By becoming aware of what the gods are trying to do to him Sisyphus can assume an attitude toward their punishment. He can either allow the gods' punishment to crush him or he can refuse to be crushed and transcend their plan for him. Once he becomes aware of his fate, Sisyphus is more than his fate. Once he understands what the gods have imposed on him, he can decide to find some meaning within his fate. Camus suggests that Sisyphus finds meaning in the physical experience of pushing the rock up the hill. Just the sheer physical experience is enough to satisfy him.

We may find it difficult to imagine how the mere physical experience of pushing a rock up a hill would satisfy someone for all eternity. We should not allow that to distract us from the main point, which is that personal presence can assume an attitude or take a stance that frees the person from any crushing or apparently frustrating experience. This is a point that needs emphasis: personal presence can transcend any situation. Sisyphus is free to take a stance or an attitude on his fate that frees him from being crushed by his fate. This is the nature of personal presence. A person is free to decide *how* he will be present. This freedom releases the person from being locked in totally by any temporal-spatial situation. Sisyphus is more than any situation in which he finds himself. This ability to transcend any temporal situation is what suggests the promise within persons.

If person is more than any temporal situation then what is the meaning of this transcendence? What direction can it take? Where is it going, if anywhere? Is there within it some hope of ultimate fulfillment? I think there is. Camus didn't. He thought that death was the end of persons. I don't. The hope of ultimate fulfillment is the promise planted within person by God. Somehow personal presence eventually will be fulfilled, not by any place but by the Presence through which personal presence comes to be. Centuries ago St. Augustine articulated this promise in writing "Our hearts are restless until they rest in you, O Lord." This century an atheist articulated the promise through his *Myth of Sisyphus*, even though Camus would never admit the interpretation of the promise which either St. Augustine or I have suggested. Within the mystery of personal presence there is a promise of God.

This book has been emphasizing that there are many ways in which a person can be present. For example a person can be present to a lecture in an interested or disinterested way, in a friendly or hostile way, in an intelligent or stupid way. How a person is present to the lecture will either open or close that person to the lecture. If a hundred persons are present in the auditorium then a hundred different lectures will be received. A hundred lectures will be received because of the types of presence the hundred persons assume. The manner of presence of each person in the audience will make that person available and attentive to the lecture in a different way. The manner of presence may reveal certain parts of the talk but also may conceal other parts of the lecture.

Loving is a way of being present. Love reveals and unveils dimensions of the loved one that other ways of being present do not reveal. Love may be the most revelatory way of being present. It reveals the depth of the loved one, the most profound dimension of the loved one. Love sheds light on the loved one in a most marvelous way. Hoping is a way of being present. It is giving infinite credit to God. It is trusting that God will lead us safely home.

Though Camus was right to say that a person can transcend any situation this should not mislead us to neglect the importance of human bodiliness. Nor should our belief that hope focuses on God as ultimate fulfillment cause us to neglect the role of hope in a person's earthly existence. We hope not as angels but as human persons. That means we hope in some place and at some time. We hope as bodily persons. Hope is incarnate.

Accepting Our Bodiliness

Trying to accept our bodiliness is tricky business. The human race seems to vacillate between two extreme views of the body: one extreme sees the body as the source of all troubles and problems, the other glorifies the body and in the process neglects the spiritual dimension of person-hood. Neither view focuses on the *human* body. Both reduce the human body to something less than it really is. The one view separates the body from the soul and attributes all human difficulties to the body; the other view separates the body from the soul, in effect denies the spiritual dimension of personal existence, and glorifies the body in the most superficial way. The first view can lead to a kind of Manicheanism and Puritanism and angelism; the second to various kinds of paganism. I think the second view is represented by some of the "peep" magazines, even those that try to assume a respectable air. One of the more discouraging contemporary experiences is to glance at a newsstand and see magazine covers with girls in various stages of undress leering out at the potential male buyer. I'm not quite sure why this type of photograph lacks appeal. Perhaps it's because the photographers and models have succeeded in presenting just a body and not really a *human* or personal body. Persons can be very attractive, but a body reduced to a thing by contemporary advertising is not alluring. Besides creating serious problems for young people, such photography can subtly lead us to treating one another as things.

In "Body as Spirit," Charles Davis wrote:

> The willingness to gaze pleasurably upon the nudes in *Playboy* or *Penthouse* and to enjoy the sight of shapely girls in bikinis on the beach is no sure sign of the acceptance of the human body. Certainly, the sight of naked feminine beauty at that fleeting stage when adolescence has just passed into maturity should give pleasure. But this, if healthy, should be a part, a relatively small part, of the full acceptance of the bodily reality of people, an acceptance with delight, but also, if total, necessarily with compassion and understanding tenderness.

The view of the body that leads to a kind of Manicheanism, Puritanism, or angelism is unfortunately often found among religious people. A scholarly study of philosophical, theological, and spiritual approaches to the body since the beginning of Christianity would probably reveal why this negative approach to the body has been so influential. I know that I have been subject to it through much of my formal education, but now I can no longer accept it. The alternative, however, is not paganism. There is the possibility of affirming the goodness of the body and yet recognizing that the self, not the body, needs mortification and ascetism. I sin, my body doesn't sin; I am lazy, my body isn't lazy; I am proud, my body is not proud.

A direct way of seeing the importance of a unified view of person, a view that sees a person as an incarnate spirituality, is to think of the Lenten season and the practice of mortification and asceticism that take place during that season. For years I practiced Lenten mortification and asceticism in order to bring my body into subjection. I thought of myself as someone who unfortunately had a body and that body was the source and cause of most of my difficulties in living the Christian life. Mortification and asceticism were done to the body so that I could use it better. I no longer think that way. I think it's closer to the truth to say "I am my body" than to say "I have a body," though neither statement is adequate to capture the mystery of human bodiliness. The purpose of mortification and asceticism is not to subdue my body but to subdue me, to deny myself so that ultimately I might be more free and open to God's saving presence. My body is not the source of my problems with living the Christian life; I am the source of my problems.

I think that my changed understanding of my bodiliness is important. The proper acceptance and joyful affirmation of human bodiliness is important if we are going to have a Christian view of our presence in the temporal order. If we think of ourselves as souls who are stuck with bodies then we can't possibly take this world seriously. Nor can we take the incarnation seriously. Nor can we allow our hope to transform our way of living. Human bodiliness is a mystery, and no religion takes human bodiliness more seriously than Christianity.

The mystery of human bodiliness holds the key to our openness to God, to other selves, and to the world. Hope is incarnate in human bodiliness. In recent years Christians have been urged to commit themselves to the ongoing redemption of the temporal order, the ongoing sanctification of the world. Some of us have been enthusiastic about the new emphasis; some quite disturbed by it. For those who see it as a complete reversal of their earlier religious training the new emphasis can be a bitter pill to swallow. I think at the heart of the emphasis is an insight into the mystery of human bodiliness.

The Mystery of Human Bodiliness

To be a human bodiliness is different from being any other type of bodiliness. To be bodily in a human way is not the same as being bodily as a chair or table. These are things. They are limited, closed in, locked in. They have very little potential. If they change they will probably change into "junk wood." The human body is not a thing. The human body is openness to others. The human body is not limited in the way things are limited. The human body, because it is a knower, can open itself to the whole world and through knowledge become the whole world.

To be a human bodiliness is not the same as being a

plant or vegetative bodiliness. While plants and vegetables grow, their type of bodiliness is also limited.

To be a human bodiliness is not the same as being an animal bodiliness. We don't have direct experience of animal bodiliness, but we can observe that they see, hear, touch, taste, and smell. We even talk about animal instinct. But there is no evidence that animals can know the way humans can know. So while animal bodiliness has more potential for growth and development than plant bodiliness or the bodiliness that things have, it does not have the potential that human bodiliness has.

Human bodiliness can relate in a knowing and loving way to others. Human bodiliness is always relating, always open to others. I presume it is clear that by human bodiliness I do not mean some reality separate from the self but rather a reality identical with the self. To be a human bodiliness is to be open in some way to others but there are many ways to be open: friendly or angrily, intelligently or stupidly, lovingly or hatefully, despairingly or hopefully. How a human bodiliness relates to other selves, to the world and to God, determines both the present and future states of that individual.

Because the nature of a self or a human bodiliness is to be open to others, it is not really possible to shuffle religion off to some special segment of the week or some section of a life experience. If I am responsible for my self or my human bodiliness then I am responsible for my relationships. How I relate to others, to the world, and to God is my responsibility. My real religion, no matter what I claim it to be, is revealed through my relationships. My lived religion, my active set of beliefs and practices, are revealed in the way I relate to other people, the world, and God. I may claim that love is the most important activity according to my religious creed, but if I don't relate to people in a loving way then my lived religion doesn't match what I profess. I may claim that God is most important in my life, but if I relate to the world in avaricious, egocentric, and selfish ways then my lived religion reveals the untruth in my statement. Religion must color all my relationships. Recently the church has emphasized that Christians should not flee the world but embrace it, not hate it but transform it, not retreat from it but lead it. No small task. But by gaining insight into the meaning and mystery of human bodiliness we can see how our vocation as persons is tied up with the world. Though it is true that we don't have a lasting city here, it is through our lives in this city that we will help bring about the kingdom of God. What reveals the importance of human bodiliness more than any philosophical reflections is the incarnation. The Son of God became human. All of creation takes on a new importance. All human relationships take on new significance and value. Jesus, through his life, death, and resurrection, reveals both the meaning and the goal of human bodiliness and the meaning and goal of hope.

The resurrection of Jesus reveals to us the importance of human bodiliness. Though we could never arrive at the truth of the resurrection or our participation in it without God's revelation, once we have received God's revelation the resurrection makes a great deal of sense. If I am an incarnate spirituality, a human bodiliness, then if I am going to encounter God in heaven it makes sense that I be there in my bodiliness. Through risen life with Jesus I will finally achieve complete human wholeness. I will be home. Until then I must hopefully work to change the world. If through grace I share on earth in the love-life of the Trinity then my hope in that ultimate union with God after death should transform my life before death.

6 Hope and Life Commitment

There are many Christian vocations. But as we look for incarnations of hope we can categorize all Christian vocations under one of three general categories: the married state, the celibate life, and the single life.

St. Paul's description of Christian marriage remains a classic.

> Husbands should love their wives just as Christ loved the church and sacrificed himself for her to make her holy. He made her clean by washing her in water with a form of words, so that when he took her to himself she would be glorious, with no speck or wrinkle or anything like that, but holy and faultless. In the same way, husbands must love their wives as they love their own bodies; for a man to love his wife is for him to love himself. A man never hates his own body, but he feeds it and looks after it; and that is the way Christ treats the church, because it is his body—and we are its living parts. For this reason, a man must leave his father and mother and be joined to his wife, and the two will become one body. This mystery has many implications; but I am saying it applies to Christ and the church. To sum up; you too, each one of you, must love his wife as he loves himself; and let every wife respect her husband (Ephesians 5: 25-33).

A Christian Marriage

In my life there are married couples who are inspiring models of what the Christian mystery means. I could use some couples with whom I have been close for years as examples of Christian hope. However I'll use a couple with whom I spent only one evening as an example because the very brevity of the time we spent together suggests the tremendous power that Christian couples have to call others to hope. In the fall of 1961 I had the opportunity to observe the various Christian apostolic movements in Chicago. That was the occasion on which I met Patrick Crowley and Patty Crowley.

When I arrived in Chicago, it was arranged that I should meet chaplains of the Young Christian Workers, the Young Christian Students, and the Christian Family Movement. Then it was arranged that I should have dinner at the home of Patrick and Patty Crowley, founders of the Christian Family Movement in this country. I remember mentioning to the person who arranged the dinner date that I hoped I wouldn't be intruding on the Crowleys' privacy. He reassured me that the Crowleys would be glad to have me. I never had a dinner experience like it before or since.

The Crowleys had decided to make their home and their lives totally open to those in need. The couple of hours I spent with Pat and Patty were overwhelming. In addition to their own children, who I think numbered five, there were two or three foreign students staying with them for a period of months. It was obvious that these students had become part of the Crowley family. I discovered that the students I met were just the latest group to whom the

Crowleys had opened their home. The students had been preceded by other students and would probably be followed by others.

During the meal I became more and more deeply impressed by the availability of the Crowleys to the needs of others. My recollection is that every time the phone rang it had something to do with the Crowleys' apostolate. I came to believe that they were totally open people, a completely unselfish couple. They were a husband and wife who had a vision of something so beautiful that they wanted to share it with the whole human race.

After supper, while Patty met with some priest about some problems connected with the Catholic Action apostolate, Pat took me into his den to discuss the CFM with me. At the time I remember thinking how strange this was: two priests being instructed by a married couple. I usually thought of priests as instructors and laity as learners. That evening was a revelation to me in many ways. I saw what being open to people really meant.

When I left Pat Crowley I told him that I hoped to start a CFM group in my parish. Over the next three years, until I went away to study, the experience of being a CFM chaplain was one of my most beautiful experiences in Christian ministry. Whatever direction or inspiration I gave as a chaplain was somehow tied up with my experience of the Crowleys. I guess I'll never forget that evening in their home.

I like to think that good actions have infinite repercussions. Somehow a good deed has an unlimited future—there's no telling how many people it will affect. If I'm right then Patrick Crowley had a great deal going for him when in 1974 he left this world to meet the Lord. He was a rather exceptional human being. He and Patty had a marriage rooted in Christian hope and they encouraged others to live lives of hope.

Christian Celibacy

In his fine book *The Sexual Celibate,* Donald Goergen in defining celibacy writes:

> I define celibacy as a positive choice of the single life for the sake of Christ in response to the call of God. There are many reasons why one might choose to be single, e.g., in order to be a playboy. To choose celibate singleness, however, is to put one's life and one's freedom in the context of a particular response to God. There are two major dimensions to celibate life: a positive choice of all that is implied in the single life as well as putting this choice in the context of the Christian vocation. One does not choose the single life for itself alone; he or she chooses it for the sake of Christ.

In some ways the title of Goergen's book is slightly misleading. The book is a theology of sexuality and covers much more than celibacy. However, Goergen's treatment of celibacy is extremely good. He has been able to get on to paper the richness of celibate existence that many have experienced but have been unable to articulate. In recent years celibacy has been under such serious criticism that Christian celibates have been bombarded and almost smothered with reasons why their particular style of living is pointless. Within the American secular community, celibacy is pretty much irrelevant. For the secular-minded person celibacy is at best a curio. Some of Goergen's insights into sexuality will help clarify the meaning of Christian celibacy.

Pointing out that both celibacy and Christian marriage are two forms of religious living, Goergen writes:

> Religious living is a specific manifestation of man's search for meaning, an affirmation that meaning is ultimately related to God. The religious person is a person who believes in God. A celibate person is one exemplification of a religious person. A person in Christian marriage is another such exemplification. The celibate person chooses to give specific witness to this spiritual dimension. As long as there are celibate people, there will be people who say by their lives that a primary motivational force in man is the desire to be one with God. The same is true of Christian marriage although Christian marriage can easily be naturalized by the culture. Celibacy resists such enculturation.

Goergen is quite right in saying that Christian marriage can easily be naturalized by the culture. This is what has happened to the vision many Christians have of marriage. A secular culture has crushed the distinct dimension of Christian marriage. This is why today, especially, preparation for marriage is so important. A Christian couple has to swim against the tide. What force is there informing and explaining to the couple the deepest dimension of their relationship? Only the church. The problem is that the church's ministers have to think of as many effective ways as possible of speaking the meaning of Christian marriage to couples. This is an enormous pastoral problem.

The church is supposed to shed light on human existence. It is trying to point to the deepest dimension of human living. Today marriage seems to be on the ropes. As an unmarried person I can only guess how difficult married life must be. I believe that within Christian marriage there are resources that are untapped. But how will married couples know of these resources unless someone tells them?

The celibate can be a help to married couples. They can also be a great help to him. Every person is called to live a life of loving. To the extent that he does, he can be a support to others. Even those whom he does not help directly can learn from him. Both the celibate and the married person can encourage one another to be loving and unselfish. Each can support the other's hope.

Goergen is correct in saying that celibacy resists the naturalization process. To put it simply, celibacy makes no sense at all if there is not a God who calls us to service. To understand celibacy at all is to understand it religiously. Goergen suggests three motivating forces for celibate existence. His articulation of these forces illustrates not only the kind of thinking that celibates should do about their own lives but the kind of thinking that married and single people should do about the meaning of their sexuality. The three forces are striving after God, striving for freedom, and striving to witness to Christian values.

By his choice of celibacy an individual tries to open himself to God. Of course, there are other ways of opening oneself to God. Celibacy is one striking way. By his celibacy an individual also wants to make God more real in the world. He is not only trying to draw closer to God but to be a sign and support to others so that God will be more real to them.

The freedom of celibacy is a freedom to be for God and to do the work of God. It is certainly not a freedom from the joys and pains of interpersonal relationship. The freedom is related to the celibate's striving for God. If a person lives the celibate life fully, he should be freed. If celibacy is not freeing him, then something is wrong. The key to celibate freedom seems to be freedom to do the work of God.

The third motivational force striving to witness Christian values, is called protest by Goergen. He's referring to what others have called the sign value of celibacy. The celibate through his celibacy protests against the culture. He calls attention to a dimension of existence which the culture misses. To a secular culture the celibate is "counter-culture." By his celibacy he is saying that God is the most important reality. He is calling attention to values that the culture does not emphasize.

Of course, striving for God, striving for freedom and striving to witness to Christian values must be part of every Christian's life. It is not just the celibate who has these values in his life or at least tries to have these values in his life. Each Christian tries to incarnate these values in a different way. The married person does it one way, the single person another, and the celibate another. In terms of examining a way of life, it is clear that Christian celibacy is foolish if it is not an attempt at incarnating these values. To the extent that these values are absent from a celibate's life, he is a bachelor rather than a celibate. His life is not rooted in Christian hope.

A Celibate Incarnation of Hope

Celibates who hope can be a tremendous support and encouragement to others. This struck me strongly during the last year when a nun I knew died. I never realized how much her hope spoke to me. I first got to know Sister when

I was teaching part time at a women's college of which she was president. In my dealings with her then and in all my meetings with her through the years she impressed me as a woman totally dedicated to Christ and his church. She seemed to be a person who had put her life together and was going in one direction. She had achieved an integrity, a human wholeness. I can't remember the last time I saw her or spoke to her, but I have the impression that on that occasion she was solicitous about my loved ones.

To me Sister was an inspiring sign and symbol of what Christian life is all about. She was so generous with her time and herself that she almost became a living legend for her interest and concern about people. It was uncanny how she would remember personal problems that were told to her or difficult experiences that people were undergoing that were related to her. Years ago, I mentioned this to a professor who taught at the college where Sister served as president. I said, "Sister is very solicitous when you mention some difficulty that someone is experiencing, isn't she?" The professor's eyes lit up. He said, "She's amazing. I might mention to her that some distant cousin of mine is sick. Months later she will say something like, 'Is Susie better?' For a moment I can't even remember who Susie is and Sister has remembered for months." Sister was hopeful and her life seemed hope-filled. After her death, story after story was recounted by those at her wake and at the funeral about how concerned she was about the suffering of others. She was so outgoing toward others that many who benefited from her kindness did not even know of her own heart trouble which had been a problem for years.

The homilist at her funeral was right on target when he described how other-directed and interested in others she was. Describing her as God-intoxicated, he said, "Nothing seemed to escape her deep interest and concern. A marriage, an ordination, a profession, an illness, a loss of a beloved one, arrival of a new baby, a promotion, an article published, a sermon well preached, a degree conferred, a spiritual or emotional problem, all took on a total new aura and dimension because we knew she cared. That is why from this day forward many will call her blessed."

When I heard of Sister's death I felt a strong sense of loss. The sense of loss I experienced was partly that the Christian community had lost such a dedicated servant. But it was also partly the real concern she showed for me and for my loved ones. I realized how much those words of concern meant to me after she died. Her hope spoke to me and called me to hope. I realized that when she died the incarnation of hope that she was would no longer be available as a support and encouragement.

Human sexuality in its physical, psychological, and spiritual dimensions must be at the service of loving. Our society doesn't seem to see this. Our culture seems to say that sexuality is at the service of the self. This is wrong. To follow this view is to shrink the self. Sexuality will only reach its fullness through unselfishness. Sexuality will only reach its fullness through hope. Christian marriage and Christian celibacy are two ways of existing through which the self can be fulfilled. Neither way of existing is easy. Unselfishness usually isn't. Both ways of existing can be living signs of hope.

The Single Life

Because I teach philosophy at a seminary, I'm frequently invited to give talks in parishes. A topic that I have dealt with frequently in the last few years, both because I am interested in it and because audiences seem to be also, is the mystery of human loving. After the talk occasionally someone in the audience asks about the application of what I have said to the single person. When the question is posed I am reminded how much the specific vocation of the single person has been neglected in most discussions of vocation.

Because of the lack of good material written on the single life, an article by Roger Repohl in *America* (11/26/76), "The Spirituality of Singleness," was especially welcome. Pointing out that the number of people living alone in the United States has risen 87 percent since 1960 and that the present strain that religious life and marriage are experiencing makes an understanding of the single life particularly important today, Repohl argues that "the fact that the single life is not a permanent commitment does not exclude it from being a valid calling from God. It is not a waste of time. It is not a mere interim state, a kind of limbo that people dwell in while waiting for God to call them to a 'legitimate' vocation. Instead, it is a calling, a commitment in itself, a way of working out one's salvation, a time of grace to be seized and shaped according to God's designs, a vital and essential membership in the Body of Christ."

Repohl makes a number of excellent points about the single person's contribution to the Christian community ranging from the single person's handling of solitude to his or her witness of hope to others. My own experience corroborates Repohl's point that single people have a special freedom to help build up the kingdom of God. For example, single people may have a freedom that married people do not have to serve in vitalizing a parish. They may not have the obligations that married people have toward family members.

Perhaps the most important contribution that singles can make today is to incarnate the Christian message into their life. They may have a power of witness that neither celibate nor married people have because of the stereotypes that miscolor their vocation. Those in celibate life are expected to live differently; those who are married are expected to follow a particular pattern and style of living. Of course, neither should surrender to stereotypes. They should constructively create their own way of living no matter how difficult that may be. Yet the single life, precisely because it is not thought of as a vocation, offers special opportunities for creativity. There are no strong stereotypes that bind the single person.

One of the most serious problems in our society is loneliness. Though not essentially connected with being alone, loneliness is often intensified in the life of a person who is not married. Many people erroneously think that marriage is the solution to loneliness. The feeling of loneliness is a feeling of being insignificant, of not mattering to anyone. It is precisely because loneliness is such a problem today that the single person can make such an important contribution. In a special way, the single person's life can speak of God's love.

One of the key misunderstandings that ought to be cleared up in the minds of both married and unmarried is that the single person is involved in the Christian apostolate because he or she has nothing else to do. In the contemporary atmosphere provided by the so-called "swinging single set" it is easy to see that singles have many avenues open to them. The image of single life presented by the "Cosmopolitan Girl" and the "Playboy" seems to suggest a life of total self-centeredness. Though the life suggested is autonomous there seems to be little in it that encourages unselfishness. The style of living promoted has no spiritual depth. It would be unfortunate if the Christian community believed that singles involve themselves in parish activities because they have nothing else to do. Singles should involve themselves in parish life because they are desperately needed.

Married couples have a unique contribution to make to parish life. However they do not and cannot have the time to contribute that singles have. Normally the vocation of marrieds demands much time spent at home. Frequently the single vocation makes no such demands. Yet singles may not wish to give their time to activities that do not deeply affect people. It is not difficult for any of us to keep busy. The trick is to be busy with something that makes a difference, something that matters, something that will really help people live the Christian mystery more deeply. There is the challenge for singles as they approach the Christian apostolate. It is also the challenge for parish leaders, clerical, religious, and lay: how to best involve people so that the Christian community will thrive and develop.

Imagining a Christian parish, some geographical area that is marked off by parish boundaries, I can think of questions that suggest important parish activities. How are the teenagers spending their time and what can be done to help them? What crimes are committed in the neighborhood and how can the police be aided in their job? What is happening ecumenically? Who are the civic leaders in the community and can they contribute to the community? What are the entertainment and recreational facilities in the community and can they be improved? What structures are deeply affecting people's lives? What, if anything, can be done about them? These are just a sampling of questions, and many more come to mind. Probably some of the problems suggested by the questions are so complex that parishioners could do little if anything about them. But others could be tackled. However, dedicated people are needed, people who can give a great deal of time, people whose basic life orientation is to help others.

The Call to Love

Every human being is called to love. Though loving takes many forms, the basic drive toward love and need for love is universal among Adam's descendants. The father of a family lives one way, the wife another, the priest another, the religious another. Each of these vocations provide obvious demands for love. The single person's call to love may not be so clear. In our society it may be blurred by the swinging single image. The unmarried Christian must carve out as clearly as possible areas in which to spend himself or herself in love. The importance of such activity should never be minimized. Rather than finding a hobby, rather than finding something to "kill time," the single person is choosing an apostolate, a mission, a way to give. The needs of people in any parish are tremendous: the single Christian can help serve those needs.

Perhaps the greatest sign value that the single person can provide is that he or she is acting freely. Not that married people, or celibates, are not acting freely in their apostolates, but so much of their apostolate is so obviously built into their vocation that their freedom is not clearly seen. The single person's freedom may be more obvious.

If a single person has no ties or obligations and freely assumes commitments and burdens to help others, that person can be a marvelous sign to others. Of course there are single persons who have numerous ties and obligations, such as caring for an elderly parent, or nursing a sick relative, or supporting nieces and nephews. Whether it is in serving relatives or serving others, a single person is called to love. When that call is answered the person is a living incarnation of hope. Such people can encourage each of us. Their hope strengthens our hope. Their courage to walk the razor's edge of unselfishness encourages us to do the same.

God has made promises that he will be present to his people. The presence of committed Christians echoes God's promise.

7 Hoping Against Hope: The Christian Life

Perhaps because I didn't make a retreat for more than a year, I recently felt the need for one. Most of my adult life, I, like most priests, have followed an annual routine of going on a retreat. For some reason which I cannot recall now, I missed one year. It's difficult to explain how I felt the need for a retreat. There was no gigantic burden on my shoulders, and I was not aware of any spiritual crisis that I was undergoing. What was on my mind was a need to "put it all together." Random thoughts had been going through my mind about the meaning of Christian priesthood, about the meaning of my life, and numerous other topics. I wanted to understand myself better, to see more clearly what I was about, and to make some evaluations and act on them. Many people must have experiences similar to mine, but they may not have the opportunity to get away and get it together.

A Religious Experience

Because I wouldn't be able to make a retreat until after the school year, I decided to make a day of recollection.

After arranging my schedule, I set aside a twenty-four hour period to spend some time in silence and recollection. The location I chose—and it has to be one of the most beautiful places on God's earth—was the seminary where I studied for six years, Immaculate Conception Seminary in Huntington, Long Island. Having made my decision to go there, I found myself, about a week or two before the day of recollection, looking forward to the day. This expectancy suggested that I really needed the day of recollection badly.

Walking the grounds of the seminary I found many memories and a few ghosts waiting for me. As I strolled the large circle that encloses much of the seminary grounds, I thought of the thousands of times I had walked it previously. Memories of other retreats, of classmates, of deceased priest friends flooded my mind. Often during the day I thought of some of my closest friends who had decided to leave the active ministry and point their lives in some other direction. I wondered about their present experience and imagined what their lives must be like, wondered about their happiness, their attitude toward the church. I also wondered about what their leaving said about my own present priestly existence. Had my friends grown in some way that I hadn't? My guess is that some of them have. Has that growth been costly and painful? I know it has. As I walked among the memories I hoped that my friends were well and happy and that in their new vocations they would be able to direct their talents and gifts toward helping people and toward building up the Body of Christ.

In my efforts to "put it all together," I began to go back over my own life—not just the past year or two but back over twenty years. I recalled my early interest in the priesthood when I was a student at Xavier High School in Manhattan, my days as a college student, my seminary experience as a seminarian, my four years as a parish priest, the years of graduate study, and the years of being a seminary professor. One truth emerged from my reflection and prayer. It may not strike others as very profound or strikingly new or particularly insightful. As I thought of all the places and especially the people who had deeply affected my life, I became aware of the active role that God has played in my life. God really has been involved. I saw that in a new way, and the truth of it is extremely important to me. In some divinely strange way, God has led me to where I am. God has been present and has kept his promises.

I don't believe in determinism or fatalism or predestination. Yet I don't believe that we are *totally* in charge of our own lives. Each human life is a dialogue, a partnership between the individual and God. Sometimes we think we can perceive God's presence more clearly than at other times. Some believers talk about this a great deal. They think they can spot God's action often in their lives. I usually don't speak that way, yet that day in the seminary illuminated portions of my life, and I became strongly aware that God has been operative in my life. Call it a moment of nostalgic experience if you wish. I call it a moment of grace. I hope such moments are experienced by many.

Two lines from T. S. Eliot's poem "Ash Wednesday" impress me: "Teach us to care and not to care. Teach us to sit still. . . ."

What does it mean "to care and not to care"? To do it calls for balance. You have to be genuinely concerned, not merely feigning interest. You have to involve yourself, lay yourself on the line. To care means to make yourself vulnerable, to allow yourself to become a victim if necessary. It means that you have opened yourself to someone or something important. You really care. Yet it also means to simultaneously not care. That's quite a trick. Though you have involved yourself there is some sense in which you keep a distance. There is some sense in which by realizing that you don't control all of reality you are ready to accept failure, or at least disappointment. If you believe in God then not caring means leaving the situation in God's hands. To care and not care is quite difficult.

Many of us go to either of two extremes. We so care that we move ourselves to the verge of a nervous breakdown. We so care that we can't eat. We so involve ourselves that we can't sleep at night. We become so preoccupied with that about which we care that we are crippled. We tie ourselves in knots.

The other extreme is that we don't care at all. We keep such a distance that we aren't involved at all. Our basic idea is that everything will work out in the end. If we believe in God we place all the problems on him and confidently claim that "God will work it out."

Hope: Caring, Not Caring, and Sitting Still

To avoid the two extremes takes some doing. If you believe in God it means-you recognize that if God is going to work things out he will do so with your cooperation. God has decided to include us in the work of redemption. God has decided to rely on our involvement. We share in Christ's redemptive work. Our freedom can make an important contribution to God's providential plan. No man is an island. We need one another. God's love often filters through people. Though ultimately our life and problems are in God's hands, God calls us to do our part. To care and not to care, to care and not be destroyed emotionally, not to care and yet to be involved: this is our vocation as persons. To care and not to care means to hope.

"Teach us to sit still." For me this line is pregnant with all sorts of applications for my life. It is also pregnant with applications for our society. We find it so difficult to be at ease. Peace keeps eluding us. Our pace of living is frantic. We are almost swallowed by the hectic flow of activities. To do nothing must be some kind of sin—at least we act as though it is. If we could be still we might be able to recognize God more easily; if we could be still we might be able to recognize ourselves more easily. If we could be still we might be able to pray more easily. Can we worship on the run? I don't think so. Worship requires composure, recollection of self. Worship requires a stillness in our being. I think worship also helps us in our attempts at being still. Worship helps us compose and collect ourselves. We get ourselves in focus as we try to focus ourselves on God.

Trying to stay deeply involved in the Christian apostolate and yet placing our trust in God is like walking a tightrope: at any moment you can lose balance and fall. The tension between trying and trusting must be sustained.

I know that charity is the most important virtue. It is the center of the Christian life. Yet hope must be right behind it. To trust in God is no small accomplishment. To say that we trust is easy. But to really trust is not so easy. I know it's a virtue I badly need. I suspect many of us do. It was certainly a virtue operative in Jesus when he was praying in Gethsemane. To deliver himself to his Father took deep trust. Jesus had never experienced death. He was afraid.

Yet he handed himself into the care of his loving Father. The Christian church must do that today.

Christian involvement requires a deep trust. If we're going to stay involved, if we're going to stay committed to Christ, then discouragement and disillusion will be frequent temptations. Anyone can be involved for a short time. Who can stay involved for the long haul? My guess is the person who trusts, who can care and not care, who can sit still in the presence of God.

Hope and Humor

In our efforts to care and not care, humor can be a great help. A sense of humor helps us put things in perspective. People who hope should be able to laugh. Hope and humor ought to be companions. This was brought home to me a couple of years ago when film director Frank Capra spoke at our college seminary.

Readers may remember that Capra was one of the most popular film directors during the 30s, 40s, and 50s. The list of films he made reads like a list illustrating "What was good about Hollywood?" Among the more famous Capra films were "It Happened One Night" (1934), "Mr. Deeds Goes to Town" (1936), "Lost Horizon" (1937), "Mr. Smith Goes to Washington" (1939) and "Meet John Doe" (1941). In many films Capra shed light on the beauty of person and the beauty of personal love.

At the college seminary the evening with Capra consisted of a screening of his film "It's a Wonderful Life" followed by a talk by Capra. "It's A Wonderful Life" is often shown on television around Christmas time. The last five or six minutes of the film may be among the most moving footage on film. In the film James Stewart plays an unselfish character, George Bailey, who has devoted his life to helping others at great expense to himself. Totally discouraged at what he takes to be his failure in life, Bailey contemplates suicide. When an angel shows him how impoverished the lives of others would have been without him, George Bailey sees that he has had a wonderful life.

During the last five minutes of the film all the people whom George Bailey has helped come to help him in his hour of need. George is overwhelmed by the love his friends have for him. The audience is also overwhelmed. The night of the screening I wondered if there was anyone in the audience who was not crying. Some critics might describe the scene as Capra-corn, but I think Frank Capra knew how to touch people. He seemed to know a special entrance into the human heart. His films are filled with hope.

Though I was very impressed by the ending of "It's a Wonderful Life," I was even more impressed by Capra's remarks. Someone asked Capra about his use of humor. The questioner pointed out that humor seems to play a very important role in Capra films, even in the most dramatic moments. The questioner wondered if this was part of some plan which Capra had. Capra was delighted with the question. He indicated that he used humor quite deliberately in his films, even in the most dramatic moments. To him humor was extremely important. His point was that a person can't laugh unless his defenses are down, and so if humor can get a viewer to relax then he is more susceptible and receptive to what the director wants to say to him.

Capra then said something that leaped out from the stage to the row where I was sitting. He said that the resurrection is the greatest comedy of all, that life should conquer death is the greatest comedy of all. The comment struck me like a beam of light.

That the resurrection is the greatest comedy of all makes life ultimately joyous. Neither tragedy nor death are the final word. Perhaps one reason that Jesus is often depicted as a clown by Christian artists is that Jesus plays the best joke against death. Though death seems to make life absurd, the resurrection makes life a happy event, a hopeful event.

If you really believe that life is a comedy then you are freed. You can face anything. The worst sufferings will not, indeed cannot, crush you if you believe that life is a comedy. There can be a kind of an abandon that characterizes your life, a certain joy of living that typifies your style of action.

Any normally sensitive adult knows that life can be profoundly sad. Sickness, suffering, and death can cast a shadow over all human experience. There is no point in denying the reality of suffering. The more honest approach is to believe that in spite of appearances sickness, suffering, and death are not the final word about human life. The final word that sums up the meaning of human life is "resurrection."

The meaning of the Easter event can shed light on everything we do. I know that I need to have more trust and confidence in God. If the meaning of Easter doesn't help me to trust the Father, nothing will. Trust is not to be confused with quietism, a heresy which says that everything depends on God and that our actions are unnecessary. The quietist opts for total noninvolvement. His vision contradicts Augustine's insight: though God created us without our cooperation, he will not save us without it.

Christian trust is active, though it's a special kind of activity, involving a gift of self.

The Easter event, more than any other event, should call us to be hopeful, trusting, and confident. In conquering death in all its forms, Jesus has invited us to give a new interpretation to all human experience. To be Easter people is to be people of hope. The Father by raising Jesus from the dead has shown that he is a faithful God. What can frighten us? To believe in Easter, to believe in the presence of the Risen Lord is to experience freedom. Once you have accepted Jesus' resurrection, what human experience can crush you?

Trusting God

Charles Peguy had a great talent for putting profound truths about the relationship between God and man into homely images. His poem "Sleep" from the collection *God Speaks* is typical of his down-to-earth practicality. Having indicated that God is disappointed with people who don't trust him, Peguy has God say the following:

I pity them. I have it against them. A Little. They won't trust me.

Like the child who innocently lies in his mother's arms, thus do they not lie
Innocently in the arms of my Providence.
They have the courage to work. They lack the courage to be idle.
. . . .
They look after their business very well during the day.

But they haven't enough confidence in me to let me look
    after it during the night.
As if I wasn't capable of looking after it during one night.
He who doesn't sleep is unfaithful to Hope.
And it is the greatest infidelity.
Because it is infidelity to the greatest Faith.

. . . .

Human wisdom says: Woe to the man who puts off what
    he has to do until tomorrow.
And I say Blessed, blessed is the man who puts off what he
    has to do until tomorrow.
Blessed is he who puts off. That is to say Blessed is he who
    hopes. And who sleeps.

Obviously Peguy is not urging us to be lazy. Rather he is
urging us to be silent within our being, to be at peace with
ourselves because we are at peace with God and with one
another. The kind of peace and silence that Peguy is talk-
ing about is not the opposite of zeal. Rather it is a necessary
ingredient of Christian zeal. Without it, zeal can become
an expression of a compulsive need to work. For Christian
zeal a trust in the Father is required. Such trust does not
necessarily reduce the amount of work you do or cause
you to lessen your efforts. Trust changes your style, your
manner of presence, your readiness to risk.

There is an oft-quoted axiom: "Work as if everything
depended on you; pray as if everything depended on
God." Taken literally, the axiom is impossible for the
Christian. The Christian knows that everything does not
depend on him. Human life and experience is a dialogue
between persons and God, and the Christian apostolate is a
project for human persons and God. Nor can the Christian
pray as though everything depended on God. The Chris-

tian knows when he prays that God wants his involvement. Prayer is never an excuse for noninvolvement. To open yourself in prayer to the Father is to open yourself to challenge and call. To trust in love takes courage because love can make serious demands.

If people's conversation is any barometer, then one of the great tasks for contemporary persons is "to put it all together." Teenagers talk about it, and so do people approaching middle age; students talk about it and so do dropouts; married couples talk about it and so do single people. We seem to have a strong experience of fragmentation. We feel we're going in different directions, and perhaps we feel as though we're coming apart. Much seems fluid. If there is any hope of putting it all together then that hope is a religious hope. To the extent that hope puts it all together it contributes to putting the person together. It helps a person overcome the feeling of fragmentation. It helps give him direction. Hope provides a person's basic direction in life.

Looking at religion in its basic meaning can provide some insights into the meaning of the Christian religion and of Christian hope. Often Christians think that their religion can be understood only in terms of ritual and law. Certainly ritual and law are part of Christianity. But there is something more basic. The Christian religion is an ultimate drive toward the Father through Christ. The vision of personal identity that Christianity provides is that the Father has called us to be his children. The vision of human community that Christianity provides is the grouping of persons under the fatherhood of God. Christianity is a person's religion to the extent that the truths are real to him, to the extent that they are the realities which drive him, which color his decisions and actions.

St. Paul summed up his own Christianity well when he wrote "the love of Christ overwhelms us" (2 Cor 5:14). This was St. Paul's real religion. To the extent that it is ours we will find our personalities changing. We will be more patient, more kind, more pure, more loving, and more hopeful. The Christian vision will not only inform us but form us. Through it, we will become new persons.

Jesus and the Promise Within Person

For a powerful and clear illustration of the promise within person, in fact for *the* illustration of the meaning of person we can look to the meaning of Jesus.

Unfortunately we sometimes think of Christian revelation as something external that is arbitrarily imposed on man. Perhaps a faulty early catechesis has given us the notion that revelation is a message from God whose meaning is less important than its source. We almost have the idea that the more confusing the message is, the better it is: the more confusing the message is the more our faith is tested. I think it makes more sense to expect from God the most illuminating message. If God gives a revelation it must contain the most profound wisdom. The promise within person is confirmed and validated in the Risen Lord. What lovers hope about their loved ones Jesus reveals through his resurrection.

A message from God should contain the most profound meaning. If we can meditate long and lovingly on the great pieces of human literature, if we can be renewed time and again by the oratorical masterpieces of great speakers, if we can plumb time and again the beautiful works of the great poets then should not a message from God be the most rewarding, refreshing, and perhaps challenging message we can receive? Jesus is God's message. Jesus is our hope. The Christ event is not merely *a* revelation from God but *the* revelation from God. The Christ-event not only fulfills our hopes and dreams but it goes beyond any person's wildest expectations. The promise within human person reaches its total fulfillment in Jesus. The carpenter's son is the fulfillment of human nature's openness. The promise we glimpse through human experience and reflection is not only fulfilled through Jesus but new promises are made through the incarnation.

People never tire of hearing the story of the first Christmas. It's been said by many that Christmas is for children. I think it's true that Christmas is for the child within us in the sense that Christmas is for the child-like hope within us. Children expect to find heaven on Christmas morning. Within the small world of the child, within the child's horizon heaven is found. The gifts that the child receives on Christmas morning are the fulfillment of the child's hopes and dreams. There is a deeper hope within human nature, a deeper promise. It may be difficult to articulate. It may go unrecognized by many. But it is there. Christmas is the answer to that hope and promise. The incarnation is the sign revealing what persons' yearnings and hopes mean.

It is up to us to freely accept or reject the promise within us, to freely follow the lead of the call within us. We can either accept or reject the mystery that we are. We can open ourselves further to God, or we can commit spiritual suicide. Whether the promise within a person is fulfilled depends on that person. He can either follow the drive within his nature toward God or he can refuse to follow it. The promise has been given us. It is within our human nature. By making us the way we are God has implanted a promise within us. To be person is to have received a promise from God.

What this promise means is beautifully and profoundly unveiled in the Christmas story. What human nature is all about can be seen in the Christ child. In the story of Christmas we find out God's plans for persons. We also find out how God keeps his promises. It is not merely that it is a lovely story that the Christmas story can be told and retold. It is not merely because it is a touching story that we never tire of hearing it. It is because it is profoundly meaningful that we can listen again and again. It is because it is in a deep sense our story that we can come to it repeatedly and be refreshed and renewed.

My story is tied up with Jesus' story. By finding out who he is I find out whom I am. By discovering Christ I discover myself. The meaning of the promise within me is tied to the meaning of Jesus' death and resurrection. The incarnation calls us to hope.

God Keeps His Promises

For centuries thinkers have been reflecting on the meaning of person and trying to correctly articulate that meaning. This is no small task. Through the incarnation we have a revelation which sheds an enormous amount of light on the meaning of person. Jesus really is a model of what human nature should be. The essence of human nature is openness to God or direction toward God. To talk about the meaning of human nature is to include implicitly the reality of God. The incarnation then is God taking to himself the nature which has a drive toward him. That human nature is openness to God is linked with the promise that person is. Ultimately the promise within a person is not in vain. A persons' yearning for fulfillment need not be a vain yearning. That personal presence is tied intrinsically to Another is why there is a promise within person. The Other can fulfill his promises, the Other can bring a person to fulfillment. This is revealed through the incarnation. St. Augustine put it well when he said that God has become man so that man may become like God.

That man is only truly himself when he gives himself away sheds light on the promise within personal presence. It turns out that the promise within person, if it is to be fulfilled, demands much of a person. The promise within a person urges him to believe that only through dying will he live, only through giving will he receive, only through unselfishness will he become a self. It has been said that person is a strange kind of treasure: only by giving the treasure away do you really find it. The promise within a person will never be fulfilled if a person is unwilling to take risks. To the extent that a person does not affirm his human nature's openness to God, to that extent the promise of person will not be fulfilled.

Personal presence is openness to God. Because of that openness, numberless opportunities arise for a person to intensify his relation with God. Personal presence is a gift from God. Divine love desires the further openness of his creatures. God wants to fulfill the promise he has planted within a person. Whether that promise is ever fulfilled depends on the individual human being. To say "yes" is to affirm God's plan; to say "no" is to frustrate it. No one has said "yes" as perfectly as Jesus. In fact his "yes" makes our "yes" possible. Jesus' "yes" to the Father is the fulfillment in principle of God's promise. Whether the promise is fulfilled in each of us depends on whether we imitate Jesus' "yes."

For Christians one of the key ways of saying "yes" is the eucharist. An act of thanksgiving, the eucharist is saying "yes" to the Father. Though we don't often think of it this way, it is also saying "yes" to who we are. It is saying "yes" to the promise within us. The eucharist is primarily saying "yes" to God, but it is also saying "yes" to the self-identity we have received from God. Each "yes" confirms that self-identity and moves the promise toward fulfillment.

The eucharistic action is a hopeful action. It summarizes sacramentally a Christian's faith and makes present sacramentally a Christian's hope. The eucharist is the sacramental fulfillment of God's promise to be with his people. Because of the eucharistic presence of the Lord, the Christian can hope.

His personal presence is God's greatest gift. The paradox of human personal presence is that it is a gift from God that becomes fully itself by being returned to the giver. A good description of person is that he is the being who can make promises. A person can do this because a Personal Presence has first made promises to him.

Questions for Discussion

Introduction

1. What does the author mean by "to hope is to become a person"?
2. What is the person explosion? Can you from your own experience give examples illustrating the person explosion?
3. Why is it difficult to know ourselves?

Chapter 1

1. What point is the author making with his anecdote about the high school entrance examination?
2. What do you mean by God's providence? How does the virtue of hope fit in with it?
3. What can we learn from the story of Job?
4. What was Jesus trying to teach his disciples when he told them to say, "We are merely servants"?
5. In explaining why a man was born blind what did Jesus mean when he said, "He was born blind so that the works of God might be displayed in him?"

Chapter 2

1. What does the author mean when he says a person is responsible for his presence?
2. Why is the *how* of personal presence especially important?
3. Is it true that the world, a person lives in is, at least to some extent, a world he has chosen? Can you explain this?
4. Why is despair spiritual suicide?
5. What can Judas and Peter teach us about hope?
6. Why is hope "the shoot, and the bud of the bloom of eternity itself"?

Chapter 3

1. What is anxiety?
2. What is scrupulosity?
3. Have you ever had an experience with scruples or some other experience similar to the author's? If you were healed, how did it happen?
4. Why is lack of meaning so harmful to personal existence?
5. Do you know any person whom you would describe as a "hopeful presence"? What about that person makes you think he or she is hopeful?
6. What is "ontological anxiety"? Have you ever experienced it?
7. What does the author mean when he describes hope as a stance toward reality?

8. What does the author mean when he describes hope as a bodily way of being?
9. Can you think of any works of art—plays, films, novels, short stories—in addition to the two the author mentions that shed light on the meaning of hope?

Chapter 4

1. Why can Abraham be called the father of hope?
2. What promises has God made?
3. Why should the coming of Jesus strengthen our hope?
4. What is St. Paul's idea of hope?
5. How was the ordination of the priest a sign of hope?
6. This week have you had any experience or observed anything that helped you to hope? If so explain what they were.
7. How does the Christian storyteller help us to hope?
8. Do you have any favorite Christian stories? What are they? Do they help you to hope?

Chapter 5

1. Why is it that to "be a person is to be in danger"? Can you illustrate with examples from your own experience?
2. What is the theme or point of the story *The Velveteen Rabbit*?
3. What does the author mean when he says that there is a promise within personal existence?
4. Does the author think atheist Albert Camus saw this promise? Why does the author think Camus articulated

the promise incorrectly? Why would Camus reject the author's articulation?

5. How is the *human* body different from all other bodies?
6. What is the Manichean view of the body? What view of the body is presented in angelism?
7. Why is my real religion revealed through my relationships?
8. How do the incarnation and resurrection reveal the importance of human bodiliness?

Chapter 6

1. What to you are the most important points in St. Paul's description of marriage in Ephesians?
2. Do you know married couples who encourage and inspire you? What is it about them that makes them so attractive?
3. Would you want to add or substract anything from Goergen's definition of celibacy?
4. Why can Christian marriage be easily naturalized by the culture?
5. What are the three motivating forces for celibacy according to Goergen? Do you agree with Goergen? Do you know celibates who have these forces in their lives?
6. Has any Christian celibate had a profound influence on your life? Can you explain why?
7. What contributions can the single person make to the Christian community?
8. The author suggests some important parish activities that would require the involvement of dedicated people. Would you add any activities to his list? Would you substract any?

Chapter 7

1. The author recounts a religious experience he had on a day of recollection. Have you had any similar experiences lately?
2. What do these lines of T. S. Eliot mean: "Teach us to care and not to care. Teach us to sit still."
3. What connection does the author suggest there is between hope and humor?
4. The author refers to "It's a Wonderful Life" as a film filled with hope. Can you name any other films filled with hope? Were they good films? Why or why not?
5. What does the author mean when he describes the resurrection as the greatest comedy of all?
6. Why does poet Charles Peguy imagine God saying blessed is he "who sleeps"?
7. Why does the author think the following axiom taken literally is impossible for the Christian: "Work as if everything depended on you; pray as if everything depended on God."?
8. How can hope help us "put it all together"?
9. What view of revelation does the author reject? What one does he suggest in its place?
10. From your own life can you offer examples of how God keeps his promises?